Why indeed are the pews empty in the Church of the 1970's? How can the institution answer the changing needs of modern man?

Everyone a Minister boldly examines new avenues of communication between clergy and laity, and the startling possibilities of a biblically-inspired Priesthood of All Believers. It scrutinizes the successes and failures of domestic evangelism and foreign missions of the last four decades, and presents new solutions for old problems—the church's role in the world and community, the pastor's new relationship to his congregation, and the continuing involvement of the laity itself.

Everyone a Minister should be required reading for every concerned Christian.

EVERYONE A MINISTER

A Guide to Churchmanship: For Laity and Clergy

OSCAR E. FEUCHT

PUBLISHING HOUSE

ST. LOUIS • LONDON

EVERYONE A MINISTER

Published by Pyramid Publications
for Concordia Publishing House

First printing March, 1974

Copyright © 1974 by Oscar E. Feucht
All Rights Reserved

Library of Congress Catalog Card Number: 73-90058

ISBN: 0-570-03184-2

Printed in the United States of America

Concordia Publishing House, St. Louis, Missouri 63118, U.S.A.

Concordia Publishing House Ltd., London, E.C. 1, England

This Book is Dedicated to
Three Great Christian Leaders

CARL FERDINAND WALTHER, pioneer church-man who developed a polity for Lutheran immigrants in America based on the priesthood of the laity;

JOHN RALEIGH MOTT, "layman extraordinary" who demonstrated this priesthood by enlisting thousands of American Christians for worldwide mission service;

L. NELSON BELL, outstanding Christian physician—missionary to China, Bible teacher and churchman, co-founder with Billy Graham of *Christianity Today*.

EVERYONE A MINISTER

This book has grown out of 25 years of work in a mission church and 25 years as a denominational secretary of adult education. Always the compelling motive has been the Biblical teaching of the priesthood of all Christians as the only adequate strategy of the church so greatly needed in the last decades of the 20th century.

Cyril Eastwood's historical review has shown that this teaching has never been fully lost by the churches *nor fully received,* and that it is time to take this basic teaching out of the slogan category.

The restudy of mission and ministry in the last three decades has led back to the apostolate of the laity. These same decades have produced a variety of helps by Christian educators and mission directors in both Protestant and Roman Catholic circles. In most denominations no adequate work has appeared. Many treatments are historical-theoretical without the practical application for our times.

In our highly organized and mechanized society it was to be expected that churches would become more and more institutionalized. The average church uses its laity in its educational and business structures. Only a few denominations have been successful in involving the laity in the ministry as the New Testament describes it and the early church practiced it.

It was this observation that suggested a more direct

linking of this teaching with the practices of the local church. However the priesthood of all Christians will remain a "paper document" until the common images of the church and its institutional structures are modified to enable church members as disciples and missioners to put into practice their Christian calling in all sectors of life and society,

I am indebted to many churches and churchmen for the contents of this book. Their insights, observations, and approaches are included to give the layman and laywoman new incentives to take a fresh look at the church; and to consider the changes necessary if the church is to become what God intended it to be: A ministerium of *all* who have Christ in their hearts.

The church needs dedicated men and women who desire deeply to get beyond nominal church membership to active discipleship, and in this way recover the dynamic power of the early Christians as described in the Acts of the Apostles.

OSCAR E. FEUCHT

June 1973

EVERYONE A MINISTER
A Guide to Churchmanship

Footnotes for each chapter are found at the end of the book.

Bible quotations unless otherwise indicated (e.g. TEV for the American Bible Society's Today's English Version), are from the Revised Standard Version.

THE CHURCH
IN TODAY'S WORLD

HAS THE CHURCH LOST ITS RELEVANCY?

The church in the 1970s is experiencing a crisis which is unprecedented in modern times. In some instances the exodus from the church is considerably larger than growth in new members. One large American Protestant denomination recently reported a loss of 40,000 members in a single year. The graphs on membership growth and church attendance of many Protestant groups of the last few years show a straight line indicating a holding operation, or they show a downward curve.

A theologian of the Roman Catholic Church reports that 25,000 priests have left the priesthood in the last 8 years and that a very large number of men and women have left the ranks of various monastic orders.[1]

At the close of 1972 the Gallup opinion poll reported that the 10-year decline in church attendance seems to have leveled off. However, the statistics on church-school enrollment and youth participation were still cause for alarm. One Gallup poll asked this question in 1967: "At the present time, do you think religion as a whole is increasing its influence on American life, or losing its influence?" The same question had been asked in 1957. Here are the responses: 1957: increasing 69 percent, losing 14 percent. 1967: increasing 23 percent, losing 57 percent. Note the very significant reversal within a single decade!

A *U.S. News and World Report* indicated that the interest of young people and young adults in the institutional church is declining in many mainline denominations. This was not the case in churches that hold to a more conservative theology. For the third year the Lutheran Council in the USA reported a 1½ percent decline in membership of its three constituent synods. Analysts think that a major factor is the apparent business-as-usual attitude of the churches and the strong emphasis on church membership rather than on Christian witness and outreach.

No church body has been unaffected by this phenomenon. Church denomination headquarters have had to cut back their domestic and foreign programs due to a reduction in church offerings. There is no doubt about it, the church is passing through a crisis.

SOME CAUSES FOR THE DECLINE

Church history shows how sociological, political, and economic factors effect personal religion and the Christian church. Each generation is subject to new and old influences. Never have these influences been so many, so penetrating, and so complex. The whole life-pattern of society has been affected. No church, no church member, remains unaffected. The spirit of modern society is not overtly antichristian. It is merely unchristian!

The factors are many: urbanization, mobility, mechanization, automation, instant world news; the transfer of services out of the home, smaller families; the science explosion and galloping materialism. Few church bodies seem to have taken into account the many changes in our culture. Social, economic, cultural, moral, and religious factors have affected our whole society. The family has lost some of its autonomy. It retains largely its affectional, recreational, social, and partly its nurturing functions, but with modern modifications.

One observer of the current scene says: "Christianity is relentlessly being pushed to the edges of a *secularized* American life, the success of the so-called conservative churches notwithstanding." Some go so far as to say that churches operating on the assumptions and patterns of the European folk-church mentality "will surely not be able to prevent the churches from becoming the *museum* everyone fears."[2]

In the light of modern books, plays, and what is aired on radio and television one critic speaks of 1972 as "the year of the cultural inversion." While in the Middle Ages and the Reformation period there was a sacralization of life, the 20th century has brought with it a secularization of life of unprecedented proportions. On the other hand, we see indications that people are presently searching for a revitalizing principle for their lives.

No church body and no local congregation can afford to go on with a matter-of-fact, business-as-usual attitude as it faces its God-given challenge to effectively minister the Gospel of Jesus Christ to the people of our modern age. This means making the Gospel relevant. If we ask: Has the Gospel lost its relevance? The answer is no! But when we ask: Has the church lost its relevance? The answer is not an unqualified yes or no. It is not because the Gospel is no longer true. It is because the institutional church in varying degrees has lost its sense of mission *through all of its members to all of its community*.

CHURCHES CAN RETOOL

A book that capsules the situation and asks the right questions, boldly and hopefully, is Albert McClellan's, *The New Times* (1968). It carries the subtitle: "A prophetic look at the challenge to the Christian church in the 1970s."[3] Its brevity is refreshing. Its forthrightness is challenging. Its relevance is evident. Its tone is positive. Its suggestions for renewal are practical. It is bold enough to say that the churches have a fatal dose of pride. It reminds us that men are changing; that we are living in a revolutionary age; that we need to discover the new individual our technology is producing; and that the church must find an effective way of reaching modern man.

He reminds us that Christians as the people of God are God's agents in today's world; that the Gospel can reach modern man and help him put things together again for a newer, fuller, more meaningful life. The church's importance and mission are greater than ever! *But the churches must retool if they would reach today's disoriented man.* The church must find man where he is! This can happen only as those who claim the name Christian become *the people of God* sent on a mission to this and succeeding generations.

FAITH IS VALID FOR OUR AGE

A mechanistic, science-oriented world is asking: "Is faith valid in a realistic age of science?" Deep down in his heart every man at one time or another has asked questions of another kind: Who really am I? What is the deeper meaning of man's existence? Who could have designed this awesome, complex universe? Why are there exact laws which enabled the astronauts to reach and return from the moon? Why is man forever seeking a higher revelation that helps him find self-identity and purpose? Why does man grasp for a hope outside of himself? How can he find peace of mind for his accusing conscience? How can he answer the problem of evil? Why does man seek reconciliation and peace?

Life has two dimensions! Christ alone supplies the way, the truth and the life! To give modern man a new knowledge of himself, a new destiny for life, a greater challenge for his existence, a way to put his life together again through faith in Jesus Christ as his Savior and Lord—that is the mission of Christianity in today's world.

ROUGH WATERS

No less an authority than Dr. Hans Küng, professor of theology at Tübingen University, Germany, in his 1972 book gives a penetrating analysis of the current situation in Christendom. He speaks of it as an emergency of catastrophic proportions. He believes the crisis ranges all the way from an inadequate Biblical foundation for the New Testament ministry to a more viable, effective, and concrete function of church members as the people of God on a mission in daily life. He sees a damaging polarity between the office of the pastors (who form "the above") and the members of the congregation (who form "the below"). He finds in the democratization of the people one of the causes of unrest in the church, and yet at the same time he sees in the democratization and activation of the people the necessary remedy. He refers to the *rediscovery and use* of the total membership of a congregation as its God-intended working force. Throughout his timely book this Biblical theologian calls for a return to the New Testament concept of the church, not as a highly organized institution but as a ministry of *all believers* witnessing to Christ in every walk and station of life. It is significant that his book carries the subtitle: "A Proposal for a New Church Ministry."

It is now apparent that the organized church is in trouble. That includes the Roman, Greek, and Protestant branches of the church tree. The malady is not a minor illness. The diagnosis may be difficult. The case has historical dimensions that embrace many centuries. The present distress involves many factors related to culture, theology, sociology, and psychology. The cur-

rent upheaval is not restricted to one or two church denominations. It is related to present-day Christendom in
an age when science and secularization preoccupy the
mind. There is unrest throughout the churches. Factors
inside and outside the churches are involved, and they
will need to be considered in any new reformations.[5]

The renaissance in the church calls for a spiritual resurrection within Christendom. This renewal must come
not only "from the top down" but also "from the bottom up." Leaders and people in every generation need
to rediscover the church as Christ's working body on
our planet. Both Protestant and Roman Catholic
churches have become highly institutionalized. We all
need to recover the spirit of the early Christians when
the church was young. The Book of Acts will need to
become again our "manual of work." All church
members will need to remember the words of Martin
Luther: "Christians are to be 'little Christs'!"

Down through the ages the people of God have con-
tinued as the holy Christian church according to the
promises of Christ, her Lord. But there have been
periods of recession and decline. History records many
incidents when the storms beat mightily on the ship of
the church. But she prevailed in the past. She will not
go down in our age or in the future. Just now she is in
rough waters!

| Chapter Two | # PROMISING SIGNS OF HOPE |

EVANGELISM ON THE MARCH

As American churches approach the 21st century they need to take a fresh look at world Christendom and learn new approaches to mission and ministry—learn not only from churches in the Northern Hemisphere but also from the fresh, new expansion of Christian witness in the Southern Hemisphere.

NORTH AMERICA ON THE MOVE

The quest for a better strategy has intensified in the last four decades. Important contributions have been made through general and special studies of the World Council of Churches and through a fresh look at the larger mission of the churches. Denominations have adopted more comprehensive plans, such as basic "Mission Affirmations."[1] New experiments in social ministries, new approaches to youth work in the churches, and relevant studies in adult and missionary education have spawned many new projects.

Young adults are volunteering for various agricultural and technical services related to world missions. Participation in linguistic work has appealed to many who give years to such services in many parts of the world. The worker-priest approach, pioneered mainly in France, is being pursued in some foreign fields and at some seminaries.[2]

The Billy Graham crusades are expanding in intensity and drawing millions of youth and adults to a new commitment to Christ and extending their operations to other countries. "Key 73—Winning a Continent for Christ" was the most auspicious evangelism project ever undertaken in North America on an interchurch basis. Its six phases were extended over an entire year: Calling our continent (1) to repentance and prayer, (2) to a restudy of the Word of God, (3) to a reaffirmation of the resurrection of Christ, (4) to recommitment to new life through various teaching ministries, (5) to the proclamation of the Gospel in every state and county of the nation, and (6) to a new commitment to cooperative witness and action.[3]

The Coral Ridge evangelism training program is being used in churches of many denominations. The training manual "Evangelism Explosion" designed and tested by its author, Dr. James Kennedy, is being effectively used not only in the training of laity but hundreds of pastors. These and similar movements represent a high-water mark for cooperative evangelism in American church history.[4]

EVANGELISM IN MIDDLE AND SOUTH AMERICA

The most significant mission history in the last three or four decades was not written in North America but south of our border, in Central and South America. This expansion came chiefly through new missionary thrusts, most of them originating outside the historic church denominations. The number of Protestant Christians in Latin America has grown from less than two million in 1945 to 19 million as of 1970. In a single year some 3,000 new evangelical congregations were formed in Brazil alone. This growth is unparalleled in the history of South American Protestant missions.[5]

The most extensive gains were made by the Pentecostal churches. One million new members were added to their churches in a 10-year period in one country. The secret of their success is attributed to immediate enlistment of the new convert in the missionary enterprise. A Brazilian Pentecostal leader cites the following factors in his report: Full participation of the people in the worship services, in reading Scripture lessons, singing, teaching, preaching, training more new converts, and in the greater use of dialog. People are made to feel at ease in the sanctuary and visit freely with each other inside the church before and after the worship service. Worship is not something you *attend* but something you *do*. Their aim is not to produce a Sunday Christian, but rather a believer who is able to witness in the society in which he lives.[6]

Mission directors attribute this unparalleled expansion to the high percentage of lay participation. The kingdom of God "is here and now" experienced in a new consciousness and expressed in concrete living. These new churches have learned to use the natural emotional strength of Latin American people in building a real, indigenous Christianity. This is the opinion of a visiting survey team which made an extensive exploratory study.[7]

There were some 750,000 Protestants in Mexico as of 1971. Less than one-fourth of these belong to the historic churches. The remainder are affiliated with newer denominations or independent groups. Lay training is emphasized in all church denominations. Augsburg Seminary, for instance, offers a 9-month course for layworkers called "Plan Seventy." Under the direction of pastors, students work at mission outposts on weekends. The oldest Protestant church in Guatemala is Presbyterian. It has distinguished itself by initiating a seminary-by-extension movement, which is now spreading throughout the younger, smaller nations. The seminary takes its program to students who work for a living during the day, study at home evenings, and meet with a professor at a nearby center over the weekend. Other denominations use Bible colleges to train a national ministerium. More and more of the Protestant churches in Central America are becoming indigenous in leadership, with guidance and training set up by mission directors from the United States and Europe. As in Mexico so in Central America the greatest growth has been initiated by the Pentecostal churches.[8]

MISSION EXPLOSION IN AFRICA

At the beginning of the 20th century the Christians in Africa were 3 percent of the total population. As of 1970 that ratio had been raised to 30 percent. This growth is accounted for chiefly by many thousands of new, independent, native African churches. In the Congo alone there were over 10,000 churches of Protestant origin by 1960, not counting the growth in Roman Catholic missions. The membership in these churches comprises one-seventh of the Congo population. It is significant that most of the new churches are indigenous. All Christian churches in sub-Sahara Africa grew from 30 million to 97 million—almost an unbelievable increase. In 1969 David Barrett predicted that by the year 2,000 Christianity will constitute 46 percent of the population of Africa, if the present growth rates continue.[9]

MISSIONS IN THE FAR EAST

When we turn toward India and the Far East, we get a few more surprises. In Indonesia some 50,000 Moslems have become Christians. The South India Conference of the Methodist Church in the face of persecution increased from 95,000 to 190,000 members. From 1955 to 1965 the Presbyterian Church in Taiwan doubled its membership.[10]

This comprehensive foreign mission review is available to us from a most remarkable new book: *The 25*

Unbelievable Years: 1945 to 1969, by Dr. Ralph D. Winter, associate professor of missions, School of World Mission and Institute of Church Growth, connected with Fuller Theological Seminary, Pasadena, Calif. This seminary complex has become the chief center for computing and analyzing world mission statistics.[11]

SOME CONCLUSIONS

It is significant that this new upsurge in missions is taking place in the non-Western churches and is lay-oriented. Already in the 19th century it was the Protestant mission societies of Europe, not the state-related churches, that initiated modern foreign missions. Led by farsighted Christian institutions and their pastor-leaders, these societies sent trained Christian workers to India, Africa, Australia, New Guinea, and other countries. These societies were largely lay-supported.

Similarly the new missionary expansion in the last 25 years has been largely lay-inspired. In fact, much of the work has been done by lay volunteers. Many independent or nondenominational organizations have supplied hundreds of workers. The Inter-Varsity Christian Fellowship, the Campus Crusade for Christ, the Wycliffe Bible Translators, the Sudan Interior Mission are a few of the organizations that now have hundreds of workers in many fields and on many continents. The Christian Missionary Alliance, the Pentecostal Church, and various Baptist churches have supplied a large number of workers. More than 200 non-Western mission organizations are supplying personnel and funds for various mission enterprises.

The greatest growth is traceable to a number of significant factors. In Africa the greatest growth came in the indigenous churches which were native to the culture and in which the laity itself was giving leadership. Success was also closely related to free, more informal types of worship which permitted more participation by the people, rather than the highly liturgical forms of the continental churches.

Another major factor in missionary success Dr. Winter traces to a viable horizontal (rather than hierarchical or vertical) organizational structure of the church where the people themselves are trained for evangelism and personally desire to win others for Christ. More and more mission boards have adopted a "decentralizing strategy" transferring leadership to the respective mission field. Vertical structures by mission boards provide perspective and direction. But it is the horizontal structure that provides the mobility for missionary outreach. Christ needs His full task forces in the field—all the people of God, not just a few "missionaries."[12]

SOME EXAMPLES

The success of the Presbyterian Church in Korea is due largely to the evangelism method devised by John Livingston Nevius. It is a built-in plan to establish *from the very start* a self-propagating, self-supporting, indigenous church. In his book *Change and the Church* Erwin L. Lueker lists the chief factors of this approach.

(1) Each man stays in his regular vocation and is an individual worker for Christ in his environment while supporting himself by his trade and work.

(2) The church organization is developed only as far as the native church is able to manage itself.

(3) The best qualified men are set aside for evangelistic work as the church is able to provide them.

(4) Natives provide their own church building in harmony with native architecture and the economic standards of the people.

(5) The method stresses extensive mission exploration into surrounding areas to reach people through personal evangelism, systematic Bible

study, strict discipline, and cooperation with other churches.[13]

The Batak church was designed to be indigenous by its pioneer founder, Ludwig Nommensen (Rhenish Missionary Society). K. Birdston describes it like this:

> You might almost say that the Batak Church stands today where the early church stood at the Jerusalem Council. A homogeneous tribal church standing on the threshold of moving out into the gentile world. It is a one-people, one-language community, but as the Christian body in Sumatra, destined to be something more.[14]

Dr. Lueker sees four basic factors in the New Testament polity of the church: (1) "All ministry centers in Jesus Christ, (2) The entire Christian community is active in ministry, (3) The ministry is given by God and is exercised through spontaneous use of special gifts, and (4) Special ministries are needed for specific situations in an evolving society."[15]

These are the promising signs of hope on the missionary horizon. In the analysis of Dr. Ralph D. Winter, "the sudden removal of Western political and military power has made the Christian faith *more,* not less, acceptable to the new nations of the non-western world." The chief mission of the church in this hour of history is its own renewal through a fuller use of its people and a fuller recovery of its horizontal structure. Christians must ever-and-again rediscover their high calling as ambassadors of Christ. In fact, *church renewal is the church's mission today!*[16]

The greatest gain in converts was not where the most money was raised but where the most Christians were at work personally winning their neighbors for Christ.

The torch seems to be passing from the older nations to the many new and younger nations, and from older churches to the younger churches. The new awakening reflects the wider acceptance of the Reformation dictum which we call the priesthood of all believers.

The task before the churches today is a task of "re-orchestration." There is a new musical score before the churches. And every member has his own instrument to play in God's symphony. It is not a new melody. The musical score was given by our Lord at His ascension (Acts 1:8-9)".

Chapter
Three

THE QUEST
FOR SOLUTIONS

INSIGHTS FROM MANY LEADERS

We have already mentioned a number of books dealing with the renewal of the church. In the last 20 years a flood of books on this subject has appeared. The output has increased since we entered the 1970s. It is important that we get acquainted with some of the most significant titles. Each book supplies some new insights. Together they form an important resource for church renewal.

Elton Trueblood has been a frequent and always rewarding contributor. Heading up the Yokefellow movement at Earlham College, Richmond, Ind., he brought out *Foundations of Reconstruction* in 1946, *Alternative to Futility* in 1948, *The Common Ventures of Life* in 1948, *Your Other Vocation* in 1952, *The Company of the Committed* in 1961, *Incendiary Fellowship* in 1967, *New Man for Our Time* in 1970, and *Validity of the*

Christian Mission in 1972. All of these refer to the enlistment of the laity in the essential day-to-day witnessing of the church. With his lectures and books Trueblood sparked a spiritual reawakening of the churches in the lives of their members, right where they are every day of the week.[1]

The Rebirth of Ministry by James D. Smart (1960) reviews the apostolic and Old Testament ministries with emphasis on making learners not merely listeners. He gives significant signals to pastors and church teachers. He writes, "Jesus was not satisfied in having a succession of audiences to which he might proclaim his Gospel; he was interested primarily in having disciples in whom and through whom his ministry would be multiplied many times over." "We must first recognize" he says, "that rarely does the church meet the world with a trained minister or theologian present to speak for the church."[2]

In 1965 Wallace A. Fisher supplied *From Tradition to Mission*. He tells the story of what he calls a dowager church which discovers the secret of new life as it moves from illusion to reality, from confrontation to response, from dialog to encounter. He then spells out the dynamics for outreach and the new fellowship which developed as members of old Trinity Church began to live together and become a working team.[3]

The Rebirth of the Laity (1962) was the title chosen by Howard Grimes to help the Methodist Church refocus its sights. He emphasized that the gathered church must become the scattered church if its members and their neighbors are to become renewed by the Gospel—a task achievable only as pastors get clear on the mission of all of God's people.[4]

In the same year, Westminster Press brought out Francis O. Ayres' *The Ministry of the Laity, a Biblical Exposition*. Its two divisions are significantly organized. Part 1: "You are A Minister"—you are called, free, sent, rich. Part 2: "Fulfill Your Ministry"—with your style of life, affirmation, awareness, responsibility, sharing, taking on the yoke of Christ. His conclusion is noteworthy: "There will never be a widespread ministry of the laity until the church changes its direction, turns from its preoccupation with self to a concern for the world, offering itself as a servant, an instrument through which God's love and justice and mercy may become operative and visible in the world."[5]

Douglas Webster in *Local Church and World Mission* (1962) pointed up for Anglicans that the world is the context of mission; that "missions" does not mean foreign missions only; that the church, wherever it is, must be the instrument of mission. The Bible is a missionary book. Local parishes can fulfill the basic mission of Christ right where they are, if the church will but accept its only conceivable form, that of a servant, not to be ministered unto but to minister, ready to wash the world's feet. A classic statement in the foreword by Kenneth Heim sets the tone: "For too long we have thought about the church and its purpose in static terms. We have tended to think of the church as a *sitting* church, the church that is waiting for something to happen. The bishop *sits* in his *cathedra,* the clergy in their stalls or offices, the people in their pews. Why is the church static? Is it because we have *domesticated* the Gospel?"[6]

With the startling title *Enemy in the Pew?* (1967) Daniel D. Walker teaches the layman how he can become literate through opportunities in his own parish (if he is more than a pew-sitter); how he can get a better grasp of Biblical theology and become an ambassador of faith—in his home, in his church, in his community—with realism and understanding. Christians *do* have something to say to the world! The church *is* at war! And the enemy can be "the spirit of irrelevancy among the church's own members!"[7]

The Gathering Storm in the Churches (1969) by Jeffrey K. Hadden reports on an extensive, penetrating research project. It uses carefully selected, precise measuring instruments. There is no make-believe in this well-documented book. It reports the attendance decline in Protestant churches, contrasts the beliefs of clergy and laity, and presents the different images of the church held by each group. Most church members believe the church is a place for solace, not for work. While Protestantism confesses the priesthood of every believer, most planning and decision-making is entrusted to the clergy. Yet the solutions lie in engaging the laity in the struggle. The opening chapter outlines three crises the American church faces. They center on meaning and purpose (what really are their goals?), belief (what is our basic theology?), and authority (who is responsible for fulfillment of mission?). The author states, "To walk away from the institution of the church is to abandon one of the broadest bases of potential support for change that exists in American society!"[8]

The Last Years of the Church (1969) by David Poling carries the subtitles, "A compassionate critique" and "God is not dead, but the church, as we know it, is dying." The author speculates on the new shapes churches will need to become spiritually and practically alive. Churches are "panting under the loads and burdens of housekeeping projects. . . . We have stained more glass and hung more drapes and gilded more crosses and plated more chalices than any era of Christendom." "Disbelief in traditional Christianity is now epidemic." "Organized religion will depend more and more on the brainpower of the layman."[9]

E. Glenn Hinson contributes a very helpful book to our symposium: *The Church: Design for Survival* (1967). After recognizing that these are disturbing days for the churches of America, this author opens windows for a clearer view of the church, the world, the mission

Christ gave the church, and the relation of the Church Universal to the local church. The church can fulfill its mission if its worship and teaching are directed at building up "The Body" and creating a dynamic nucleus, which pours out its life in service to the whole wide earth. He recognizes that no function is so neglected as the preisthood of believers. The church can restore it only by making religion more than a creed recited in a church service. The whole program of the local church needs to be refocused so that people in all situations of life are confronted with the reconciling Gospel *in the idiom of today.*[10]

Security and mission in conflict is the problem approached by Donald L. Metz in *New Congregations* (1967). The author demonstrates how a congregation undermines its *formal, basic goals* (fellowship, nurture, service) while achieving its *survival goals* (gaining members, erecting buildings, work among members), thus becoming an organization rather than a fellowship of believers on a mission. He sketches six different church-operational patterns in six varying communities. This book will help you rethink your church's essential formal goals, recognize the negative pressures you are under to keep them *above* mere survival goals, and what you can do if a stalemate develops. A most significant analysis![11]

The Integrity of Church Membership by Russell Bow (1968) reminds us that church renewal must come *from within.* It shows: how church members lose Christian integrity; the basis for genuine discipleship; that integrity must be built in at the point of entrance; and that personal spiritual growth should be continuous from birth to maturity. The last chapters deal with the painfulness of discipline and how to develop *membership-for-mission.* Traditional, cheap church membership can be turned into authentic, personal Christianity through recovery of *discipleship.* Here is a sound analysis and a proved solution for church renewal. He asserts, "Integrity of membership requires live births—dead babies don't grow. It requires spiritual nurture—abandoned babies soon die." This pastor wants more than "paper members."[12]

Beyond Enchantment by M. E. Johnson (1972) helps us see many different people who come to church for quite different reasons. It explains why some soon drop out; why many are members in name only; what some are looking for and do not get; and causes which contribute to decline in church attendance and membership. Many church members have only inherited beliefs, others follow the passivity pattern so common in most churches. The church needs to become a two-way street! The criticisms of the church by today's society can jar your parish out of its complacency.[13]

Robert S. Clemmons contributes a very positive and constructive book. It deals with renewing adult members and bears the title *Education for Churchmanship* (1966). Do church leaders want the laity to be institutional maintenance men who help the preacher run the church? Mere spectators? Only supply financial resources? Every member should be asked: What does *being* the church mean to you? Christ asks for the reorienting of life. And this cannot be achieved without an adequate definition of discipleship, participation in lifelong learning and servanthood. This implies passing on the grace of the Gospel in all possible ways—by testimony and life. The Christian must *be the church* in all arenas of life, know the Bible not as a story book for children but as a manual of arms for the Christian's mission in his everyday world. There must be no freezing of clergy-laity relations as in the Middle Ages. The Reformation lit a torch of new freedom and new responsibility.[14]

Cycles of Renewal, Trends in Protestant Lay Education (1969), by William M. Ramsay calls attention to

churches which have been renewed by courageously re-
thinking the mission Christ gave His followers and developing the disciplines for its achievement in our modern world. He cites the example of the Church of Our
Savior in Washington, D. C., which gives a *two-year*
course to new members to equip them for active discipleship and on-the-job witnessing. "The present institutional structure of the church must give place to new
structures that will *be the church on mission,*" says Pastor Gordon Cosby, who believes that present structures
are no longer renewable. This book outlines two major
tasks of today's churches. The first is called "Journey
Inward"—to help members see themselves, to confront
their own sins, and to yield to the radical claim Christ
makes upon them. The second task is the "Journey
Outward"—to help members be in mission in their
world; day by day exemplifying their faith out in the
world wherever they are. Renewal cannot come without
new curricula for adults. Examples and resources are
suggested.[15]

Erwin Lueker's 1969 book, *Change and the Church,*
has a world-mission perspective. A study of non-
Western churches suggests some basic conclusions: (1)
Whenever "church planting" rather than Christ becomes the chief focus of concern, distortions of church
and ministry result. (2) Whenever the instrumental
character of church and ministry is overlooked, wrong
emphases immediately result. (3) When solidarity becomes an end in itself, an "in-group" results. The individual becomes insulated from the world. (4) When a
church becomes obsessed with self-preservation it loses
its role in the world. (5) When interest in humanity and
the world is replaced by interest in self-structure, institutions become the remnants of functions. (6) The life
and crises of young churches cause us to examine anew
the traditional forms of church and ministry. (7) Many
younger churches (Japan, India, Korea) have shown

that physical facilities are to be constructed for full-week use and not merely for an hour's worship. His four basic conclusions are: (A) All ministry centers in Jesus Christ, (B) the entire Christian community is active in ministry, (C) the ministry is given by God and is exercised through the spontaneous use of special gifts, and (D) special ministries are needed for specific situations in an evolving society.[16]

Were I asked to choose one book from the many titles in this category, it would be Robert C. Worley's 127-page *Change in the Church: a Source of Hope.* It is the result of an in-depth study. The chapter titles give an overview: (1) Rugged Individuals or Churchmen? (2) The Church as a Dynamic, Interdependent Institution, (3) The Character of the Church as Organization, (4) A Living Body or a Dismembered Corpse? (5) Toward a Theology of the Institutional Church, (6) and (7) Toward an Understanding of Organizations, (8) Clergy and Laity—Agents of Institutional Change, (9) Transforming Church Organizations. This book avoids the radical approach of full demolition and an entirely new structure. It realizes that churches must begin where they are with the metamorphosis which the Gospel can supply. It deals realistically with the changed new world in which churches must operate and shows the approaches they can make which will lead to genuine renewal. Like almost all of these books, it recognizes the priesthood of every believer as the core principle.[17]

The church that lives only on the traditions of the past without recovering this Biblical concept for each new generation of its members will stultify. It will continue to operate without using the dynamic principle of really being the chosen people of God, alive in Christ with a challenging mission—a mission that can be fulfilled only by the participation of its members who are consciously the body of Christ.

THE PRIESTHOOD
OF ALL BELIEVERS

ITS REDISCOVERY AND BIBLICAL BASIS

The Christian church is more than a number of worldwide church denominations with intricate organizational structures. It is the sum total of all who believe that Jesus Christ is Savior and Lord. It comprises all who confess "the holy Christian church the Communion of saints" (Apostles Creed) or the "one holy Christian and apostolic church" (Nicene Creed). The church is all persons "called out" to be God's people on mission for Jesus Christ. It includes the isolated little clusters of Christians in the mountains of New Guinea, new mission stations in exploding Africa, and Christian congregations in the capital cities of the world.

This church has been commissioned to carry Christ's mission down through the ages in constantly changing cultures. The 20th century, like the preceding centuries, has seen the rise and fall of many nations. Civilization has expanded in our own lifetime at so rapid a pace that no person can get a full grasp of the many changes and their full meaning for the human race. *This gives our generation the stupendous task of continuous reorientation.*

It is not too different in Christendom. Our century has observed the development and decline of what was called "theological modernism" in the 1920s, the upsurge of the churches after World War II, and the debate over old and new theologies in the 1950s and 1960s. The church will continue to face new problems in the field of Christian doctrine and ethics. There have been periods of recession as well as bold and promising movements of renewal throughout its long history. The church must always be in the process of self-renewal through the dynamic power of the Gospel if it is to be relevant to the modern world to which it has been sent by its Lord.

A PEOPLE'S CHURCH

A significant fact in the modern church is that it is becoming in various degrees a "people's church." Christians who are alive to the life-changing challenges of the Gospel are not satisfied to be only names on a church membership roll. They see themselves as part of Christ's working force in today's world. They have some of the same spirit which activated the first converts and sent them into Asia Minor, Africa, and Europe to make the Gospel known.

The call today is, "Christians come alive!" "Practice the priesthood of all believers!" J. B. Phillips, in introducing his translation of the Book of Acts *(The Young Church in Action)*, says of the first Christians:

> These men did not make acts of faith, they believed; did not say their prayers, they really prayed. They didn't hold conferences on psycho-somatic medicine, they simply healed the sick. . . . But if they were uncomplicated by modern standards we have ruefully to admit that they were open on the God-ward side in a way that is almost unknown today. Consequently it is a matter of sober history that never before have any small body of ordinary people so moved the world that their enemies could say that these men 'have turned the world upside down'.[1]

The Book of Acts is the best documentation of the

priesthood of all believers and the chief resource for its recovery in our day. It is true that we live in a very different age. Many historical and social forces separate us from early Christianity. During these 1,900 years the church has become more and more organized. It has been influenced by many factors, chiefly by its institutionalization and connection, at least in part, with the state in many countries across many centuries.

THE 'UNIVERSAL' PRIESTHOOD

The leaders of the Protestant Reformation rediscovered and redefined the role of the laity as all of God's people involved in the life and mission of the church. The theologian-historian Philip Schaff refers to Martin Luther as "the chief leader of the Reformation which carried Christendom back to first principles, and urged it forward to new conquests."[2] Luther championed the general priesthood of believers. "This principle," said Schaff, "implies the right and duty of every believer to read the Word of God in his vernacular tongue, to go directly to the throne of grace, and to take an active part in all the affairs of the church according to his peculiar gift and calling. . . . The principle of the general priesthood of the Christian people is the true source of religious and civil freedom."[3]

It is interesting to know that all church bodies are not only heirs to this truth but also apply it today in various degrees. Especially significant is the more recent emphasis on the "apostolate of the laity" in the Roman Catholic Church.

"From justification by faith, it is an easy step to the universal priesthood of believers," wrote William Dallmann in a commemorative essay on the 400th anniversary of the Reformation. "The Old Testament distinction between priest and people, clergymen and laymen, is at an end. Christ, our high priest, has made all Christians priests unto God. All Christians are God's clergy, and so there is no special clerical order in the church. The ministry is an office, not an order, much less a threefold order of bishops, priests, deacons. . . . The church is a government of the people, by the people, and for the people, and all Christians are the people."[4]

Another contributor, C. Abbetmeyer, wrote: "The external organization and administration of the early church was such as befitted the royal priesthood of God's children. In that community of brethren all were of equal dignity. Each member had for himself access to the Word and heart of God, and to all conjointly had been given one office, the ministry of the Word."[5]

Through the centuries since the Reformation many prominent leaders in world Christendom have reissued the call for a functional use of the laity in the life and mission of the church. "A church which proclaims the priesthood of all believers but does not in fact provide ways for the general priesthood to express itself will teach not initiative but docile obedience as the Christian stance," says Franklin Littell.[6]

In his book *Your Other Vocation,* Elton Trueblood writes: "If we should take lay religion seriously as was done in the early Christian church, the dull picture presented by so many contemporary churches would be radically altered . . . pastors would not be performing while others watch, but helping to stir up the ministry of the ordinary members."[7]

William A. Danker, a professor of missions, writes, "One of the most important functions we need to recover and use in the church of our time is the apostolate of the laity. There are fronts of Christian witness where only the laymen can make a testimony. Occupational evangelism is being stressed on both sides of the Pacific."[8]

Under the title *The Tragedy of the Unemployed,* R. C. Halverson puts the call to the laity strikingly: "The authentic impact of Jesus Christ in the world is the collective influence of individual Christians right where they are, day in, day out. Doctors, lawyers, merchants, farmers, teachers, accountants, laborers, students, politicians, athletes, clerks, executives . . . quietly, steadily, continually, consistently infecting the world where they live with a contagious witness of the contemporary Christ and His relevance to life."[9]

THE BIBLICAL BASIS

The priesthood of all Christians rests on a solid Biblical base, both in the New Testament and in the Old Testament. But this basic doctrine must be rediscovered by every new generation of Christians! Negatively stated, *it can be lost in a single generation.* Unfortunately it is often completely bypassed in Christian instruction or treated so slightly that the new convert does not get a clear grasp of it or understand its practical implications. Pastors and teachers would do well to reexamine the church's teaching and training curricula and programs for all age levels, childhood to adults. *Just where, when, and how is the "priestly" image given to all members of the parish to which you belong?*[10]

Let us now explore what the Scripture teaches on this point. The classic Bible passage is 1 Peter 2:4-10: "Come to the Lord, the living Stone rejected as worthless by man, but chosen as valuable by God. Come as living Stones, and *let yourselves be used* in building the spiritual temple, where you will *serve as holy priests,* to offer up spiritual and acceptable sacrifices to God through Jesus Christ" (TEV).

The next three verses (6,7,8) are quotations from Isaiah 28:16, Psalm 118:22 and Isaiah 8:14. They indicate that the rejection of Jesus, His suffering, death, and resurrection were all part of God's great plan for salvation predicted by the Old Testament prophets. These have now been fulfilled. He who was rejected of men has become the Cornerstone of the church. And all *believers have become living Stones built into that temple.* Christ is the Cornerstone. The Holy Spirit is the Architect. The Christians themselves are building blocks. In verse 5 the figure of speech changes. *The believers are the priests* offering themselves to God in daily service, in their "wholeness," that is, in all that they are, do, and say. This classic passage can best be described as a montage in which many pictures of the Christ and the Christian are assembled on one colorful poster.

Verses 9 and 10 develop the priesthood concept more fully: "But you are the *chosen race,* the *King's priests,* the *holy nation, God's own people,* chosen to *proclaim* the wonderful acts of God, who called you from darkness into His own marvelous light. At one time you were not God's people, but now you are His people; at one time you did not know God's mercy, but now you have received His mercy" (TEV). It should be noted that the term "God's people" is itself a *functional term!*

No less than six titles are given to the Christian in 1 Peter 2:5,9. They are based on Old Testament promises and figures of speech. According to this catalog of titles every Christian is claimed by God, belongs to a holy nation, is set apart for a particular ministry, has both a "kingship" and a "priesthood" of his own to fulfill in his life. It is significant that these are the words of the apostle Peter, one of the three disciples closest to our Lord. These titles raise all believers to the status of "ministers." They put all Christians in the role once performed by Old Testament priests. The coming of Christ brought to the church a whole new dispensation, a new order—an order of the *laos* including every Christian, both man and woman. "So there is no difference between Jews and Gentiles, between slaves and free men, between men and women: you are all one in union with Jesus Christ" (Galatians 3:28 TEV).

This teaching is not restricted to this one basic reference. Just as significant is the apostle Paul's description of all believers as "fellow-citizens with God's people," as "members of the family of God," as part of a "growing" temple of God, "built together into a sacerdotal temple" (Ephesians 2:18-22 TEV). That these terms are more than metaphors becomes clear in Paul's letters to the early church.

For this ministry of the *whole church* the Holy Spirit has bestowed on *every* Christian various gifts. The apostle Paul uses a whole chapter to expand this concept (1 Corinthians 12). "For Christ is like a single body, which has many parts; it is still one body, even though it is made up of different parts" (12:12 TEV). The diversity of gifts is given for the *mutual* profit and well-being of *all* Christians. *In this one body the interrelationships and mutual helpfulness are to be as cooperative and complementary as the various members and organs of the human body.* (12:14-27).

We can better understand the mutual services God intends for the members of His body by the intricate workings of the brain and the human nervous system, more complicated than the modern computer. Think of the automatic functions of the organs of digestion and the assimilation of the food we eat, or the operation of the heart and the bloodstream through its arteries and capillaries. It is most significant that the apostle chose the human body as the ever present example of the interaction and mutual helpfulness of Christians in the community of the church.

The embodiment of the Christian takes place in his baptism. In this way Paul summarizes the fact that the Christian in his totality, with all his talents and potentials, is to be employed in God's service. "So then, my brothers, because of God's many mercies to us, I make this appeal to you. Offer *yourselves* as a *living* sacrifice to God, dedicated to His service and pleasing to Him"

(Romans 12:1 TEV). Paul practiced this in his own life. "I am a free man, nobody's slave, but *I make myself everybody's slave* in order to win as many as possible . . . so I become all things to all men, that I may save some of them by any means possible" (1 Corinthians 9:19-22 TEV).

FULFILLING THE OLD TESTAMENT

There is a unique correspondence between the Old Testament and the New Testament regarding the priesthood of *all* believers. The terms used in the classic passage in the First Epistle of Peter are taken chiefly from the Old Testament texts such as Exodus 19:6 and Deuteronomy 14:2. God chose men like Abraham, Moses, and Joshua to gather and lead His people. The prophet Jeremiah speaks of a new age for all the people of God. "I [God] will put My law within them, and I will write it upon their hearts; and I will be their God, and they shall be My people" (Jeremiah 31:31-33). The Book of Hebrews indicates that the old Testament rites were temporary *until all of God's people would form the priesthood of the new covenant* (Hebrews 8:8,10).

The 12 apostles take the place of the 12 tribes of Israel to give continuity to "the *people* of God" (Acts 2:39; 3:25). The ministry of John the Baptist was "to make ready for the Lord *a people prepared*" (Luke 1:17) in fulfillment of Malachi 4:5-6. The apostle Paul in 2 Corinthians 6:16 quotes Ezekiel 37:27. "*I* [the Lord] *will live in them* and among them, and I will be their God and *they shall be My people.*" In his letter to Titus he speaks of Christ "who gave Himself for us to redeem us from all iniquity and to *purify for himself a people of His own* who are zealous for good deeds" (Titus 2:14).

Isaiah predicted the New Testament era when *all* of

God's people would be His servants: "*You* shall be called *the priests of the Lord,* and men shall speak of you as the *ministers of our God*" (61:6). When two persons who were not priests prophesied in the camp of the Israelites, Moses was asked to censure them. Instead he replied: "Are you jealous for my sake? Would that *all the Lord's people were prophets,* and that the Lord would put His Spirit upon them" (Numbers 11:26-30).

THE WITNESS OF PAUL AND JOHN

In his extended dissertation on the use of the gifts of the Holy Spirit, Paul says: "So we, though many, are one body in Christ, and individually members one of another. Having gifts that differ . . . let us *use* them" (Romans 12:4-6). "Do you not know that you are God's temple?" (1 Corinthians 3:16). God does not live in man-made shrines or buildings but in persons! The Christian heart is God's altar.

The Book of Revelation at a number of places echoes the priesthood of every Christian. God "loved *us,* and by His death He has freed *us* from our sins and *made us a kingdom of priests* to serve His God and Father" (1:5,6). In his vision of heaven John sees people "from every tribe, and language, and people, and nation," whom God has made "*a kingdom of priests* to serve our God" (5:9-10). At the great awakening which we call the resurrection, the faithful believers "shall be *priests of God* and of Christ, and they will rule with Him" (20:6).

It is unmistakably clear that the term "priest" as used in the New Testament does not refer to officiants in a church building but describes all Christians in their role as the priesthood of all believers.

Chapter Five

RECOVERING A RICH HERITAGE

HISTORICAL SURVEY

The Scriptures use many names, titles, similes, and parables to describe the church and its members in addition to the terms already mentioned. A great many refer to the functions of members of Christ's body. Among these are: God's plantation, the olive tree, vineyard and vine, salt, light, leaven, kingdom, fellow soldiers, stewards, servants, the chosen, one flock, God's temple, people of the Way. In his book *Images of the Church in the New Testament* Paul S. Minear refers to 53 Old Testament passages and 772 New Testament verses that enrich our understanding of who we are and of our mission in the world. No less than 96 analogies to the church are treated.[1]

No modern writer has contributed more to the fuller understanding and application of the priesthood of all believers than Cyril Eastwood, an English Methodist, in his book *The Priesthood of All Believers*.[2] It traces the understanding and application from Reformation times to the present day. No other work is so comprehensive and so well documented. The reader is amazed at the germinal nature of this teaching in the formation of many denominations of modern Christendom. This book contains extensive chapters on its influence in the life and work of Martin Luther, of John Calvin, the Swiss reformers, and major divisions of Christendom.

The universal priesthood demanded a new look into the ecclesiology of the Anglican-Episcopal church. It is also expressed in the presbyterial form of government, was more prominent in the thinking of John Wesley than is commonly assumed, and was a fundamental concept in several divisions and movements of the Puritan traditions, including the Congregationalists, Disciples, Friends, Quakers, and the Baptist churches. John Wesley saw clearly the relation of justification by faith to the concept of the priesthood of the laity. Luther said that worship and vocation flow from one font. *This priesthood is the connecting link between the dying Christ and dying men*.

John Calvin applies to believers all the characteristics and functions of priests which he found in the Old Testament. "Holy as chosen by God (1 Peter 1:2,15), sprinkled with sacrificial blood by accepting Christ's sacrifice (Hebrews 12:24), washed with pure water in baptism (Hebrews 10:22), dedicated with the laying on of hands (Hebrews 6:2), anointed (1 John 2:20), taught as they themselves are to teach (1 John 2:27). They offer sacrifices, good works, prayers and praises (Romans 12:1; Ephesians 5:2; Hebrews 4:16; 13:15).[3] This is well supported by the other Reformation leaders.

The pastor exercises a priesthood which *all* Christians possess. It is carried out *not instead* of the people but *alongside* them, *with* them but *not for* them.[4] If the Gospel is to reach all mankind, it must be preached by every person who has received it.[5] The modern welfare programs and social consciousness are a direct result of this teaching.[6]

The whole work of the church was set in a broader context. Understanding the doctrine meant privilege, but with it came also a set of responsibilities. Nowhere was this more tangibly expressed than in evangelism, in home and foreign missions.[7] The Congregationalists' concept of the church drew very strongly on the priesthood of the laity.[8] It emphasized Luther's position that *ministry is set within the church and not above it.*[9]

The Baptist churches built their practical theology on the mediatorship of Christ as Prophet, Priest, and King. John Smyth during his exile in Holland became the founder of the first English Baptist Church. His five basic principles draw on the priesthood of all believers:

(1) The faithful through Christ are made spiritual kings, priests, and prophets and have an anointing from the Holy One (Acts 1:5; 1 John 2:20).

(2) The saints as priests offer up spiritual sacrifices acceptable to God by Jesus Christ.

(3) The actions of the priesthood of the saints are actions of concord and spiritual worship.

(4) The brethren jointly have all power both of the kingdom and priesthood immediately from Christ (1 Peter 2:5; Matthew 18:20).

(5) In the absence of an "elder" a congregation nevertheless has the power to preach, pray, administer the sacraments, and perform other functions of ministry.[10]

The ideal church, says a Methodist history, "does not consist of an active few, the ordained clergy and the passive many, the laity who are just content to be the recipients of benefits from the clergy: *All are called to serve* in the church of Christ."[11]

TWELVE SUMMARY OBSERVATIONS

In his introduction Cyril Eastwood says the doctrine of the priesthood of all believers needs to be *"taken out of the slogan category* and set in its true context as an essential and *determinative* element in the theology of the Church." He shares 12 significant summaries in his conclusions.[12]

(1) "No single church has been able to express in its worship, work, and witness, the full richness of this doctrine."[13]

In this first statement Dr. Eastwood widens our vision and stretches our imagination. Almost all bodies in Christendom have profited much from the rediscovery of the priesthood of all believers. False dichotomies like sacred/secular, priest/layman have prevented a proper grasp of this call to *all* God's people. So also has the further institutionalization of the church in recent decades.

On the other hand, never before have the general circumstances for the implementation of this principle been more favorable. The raising of the entire level of education and the revival of the concept of Christian vocation are a challenge to the churches. The Bible, now available in more languages and enjoying wider distribution throughout the world, undergird the lay ministry. The new creativity and resourcefulness of Christian leaders today are favorable to a rebirth of the ministry of the laity.

(2) "The doctrine has been a living issue in each century since the Reformation."

Theologians of every church body are reading such classics as Hendrick Kraemers' *A Theology of the Laity*. Ecumenical conferences have emphasized mission and ministry more in the last several decades than any period since the Reformation. The priesthood of all believers remains not only a live doctrine for any New Testament ecclesiology, it supplies the dynamics for action in our times.

(3) "The doctrine is a unitive, positive, and comprehensive principle which springs directly from the evangelical concept of 'free grace.' "

The whole ministry of the church is set *within* the universal priesthood. The concept of the "people of God" flows as one stream through Old and New Testaments and gives the whole church on earth a single, divinely appointed, corporate mission. It was historically the only priesthood in the first two centuries of the

Christian era. It culminates the service of the Old Israel, links it to the coming of Christ and to the creation of a New Israel. It springs naturally from the chief principles of the Reformation: *sola scriptura, sola fides, sola gratia.* It is a consequence of "free grace" *and is its only adequate outlet!*

> (4) "The doctrine affirms that the divine revelation is more important than the means which God uses to mediate it."

The rediscovery of the priesthood of all believers placed the emphasis on the *Gospel message* not on the forms of institution and rites of worship. The Gospel is not merely to be preserved, but *passed on*—in a human chain of command—by living conveyors. Not the church's structure, nor its canon law, not even the written Word are the end and purpose of the church, but *the handing on of the Gospel to the end of time.*

> (5) "The doctrine is an assertion that God's justifying activity is proclaimed in the lives of all believers."

Justification by faith states the believers reconciliation and relationship to God. The priesthood of the individual Christian expresses that relationship to his fellow man. In point of time the Gospel is to be relayed all the way from Calvary to the return of Christ. "There can be no higher conception of priesthood, and it is the privilege of *all* the followers of Christ." Christians themselves are the New Israel (Jeremiah 31:31-34). A separate order of priests is an ecclesiastical innovation more related to the Old Testament than to the New Testament ministry.

> (6) "The doctrine is intrinsically related to the High Priesthood of Christ."

The church father Polycarp (A.D. 69-155) echoes the belief of the post-apostolic period when he says: "There was now the same High Priest and Mediator for all, through whom all men, being once reconciled unto

God, are themselves made a priestly and spiritual race."
Eastwood drives this point home by reminding the
church that she has often forgotten or neglected this
teaching *and when she forgot she was less sure of her
mission* and *less able to fulfill it.*

(7) "The doctrine is significant for an under-
    standing of the word 'ministry.' "

Ministry has been given by Christ to the church, to
be exercised *in* the church, *for* the church, and *by* the
church. The church does not exist for her own purpose
but only as the *servant* of Christ. *All* members of the
church are called into this priesthood. Once understood,
millions of today's "church members" would have to
radically change their self-understanding of what it
means to be a Christian. *Christ is manifest today in His
serving followers.* In the footwashing in the Upper
Room Christ Himself demonstrated this to His disciples.

(8) "The doctrine is significant for current Ecumen-
    ical Studies."

Only believers in Christ—but all believers in Christ
—form the one holy Christian church we confess in the
Apostles' Creed. All of these are members of the one
body. All are incorporated into Christ. All have been
given new life by the Holy Spirit. All have no other
Lord than Christ. All receive the same commission He
gave to the believers on the mount of the ascension. The
church of Christ is universal. The priesthood-of-*all*-
believers concept underscores our Christian doctrine
of the church. To *be* that church, we must be *living* witnesses to Christ. The Gospel belongs to all Christians. *It
becomes visible when God's people are on a mission
where they are!*

(9) "The truths inherent in the doctrine should be
    incorporated in the worship life of the church."

Some people go to church primarily to hear a preacher, as if the rest of the service is merely to be endured.
Dr. Eastwood advises that the orders of service should

change passive onlookers into active participants. Most people who have fallen in love with the liturgy have fallen in love with a "form" that may have less rather than more meaning with each repetition. We should welcome the remodeling that is presently going on in worship services, especially new participation devices. Well chosen new worship forms can help restore the fact that the believers form a fellowship of the concerned—a chain of command that begins with Christ and that is passed on by the pastor to his people, who then relay it to their neighbors and friends during the week. Corporate worship is just the beginning. It is not the fulfillment most churchgoers believe it to be. *It is a commissioning! Not a dismissal!*

(10) "The doctrine anticipates the full participation of all Christians in the evangelistic action of the church."

No pastor can fulfill the ministry God gave to each believer. Unfortunately centuries of erroneous thinking in the church has made the tasks of 500 parishioners the task of a single pastor. It was not so in the early church. They who believed went everywhere preaching the Word. There is no concept that can reverse this error in the churches more effectively than the priesthood of all believers. The question is: How can they recover what they never really possessed? The priesthood teaching is a dead document unless it is inscribed in each believer's heart. This can be done only as it is taught specifically to each new and old member of the parish. The spiritual life and mission of every parish is at stake here. It is when the whole parish with all its members is committed to the task of evangelism that something exists which no force in the modern world can stop. The challenge is to mobilize the full manpower and womanpower of the church for evangelism.

(11) "The doctrine leads to a fuller understanding of the doctrine of divine vocation."

Luther and Calvin agreed, says Eastwood, that there is only one "divine vocation" for all Christians who accept their role as the people of God, to be exercised in various spheres of life. The convinced Christian cannot tolerate a split personality idea in his life. The Christ in our hearts want to express Himself in the totality of our lives, in service to others wherever we are, in whatever we do. The Christian, who understands that commitment to Christ involves all living, enlarges and enriches his whole life.

(12) "The eschatological significance of the doctrine."

The anticipation of being with Christ forever and reigning with Him (Revelation 20:6) gives the Christian a sense of direction, the drive of hope, the joy of anticipation. Everlasting life will be the final "crowning" (Revelation 2:10) and "fulfillment" of the Christian priesthood. Nothing less is promised by Christ. *Our earthly priesthood is not exercised by folding hands in anticipation of heaven.* On the contrary, it is demonstrated by activity, witness, mission, service; *by walking in Jesus' shoes!*

Cyril Eastwood capsules this penetrating study in the following sentences:

> Every function of the members of Christ's body is a ministry; and Christ Himself is the primary holder of every ministry. This implies that all Christians are known by one word: *servant.* God rules through those who serve. There is no other way. Christ continues His ministry through His people.
>
> The church does not exist for her own purpose but only as a servant of Christ. She serves God's purpose, but must never control it. She serves the world, but must never forsake it. Servanthood is the key to priesthood.
>
> This service, however, is an obligation; and no one may contract out of it. It is the priesthood of all

believers and not merely some. So having received the benefits of Christ's Passion, the believer goes forth into the life of the world to render to Christ that form of service or that ministry for which God has equipped him. But all are expressions of the same priesthood, and one is not more important than the other.[14]

A ROMAN CATHOLIC VOICE

Several references have already been made to Hans Küng's 1972 book *Why Priests? A Proposal for a New Church Ministry*.[15]

Every pastor and layman who wants to find a positive answer to the current decline in the church should make this book priority reading. It is a must for local church boards and denominational leaders.

Dr. Küng is a Roman Catholic theologian. His voice is listened to in today's Christendom. He has been criticized by the Vatican, but looked up to by Catholic and Protestant churchmen because he is fundamentally a Biblical scholar. He approaches the Bible objectively and can cut across the traditions of centuries to get back to basic Christian theology.

The author concedes that the church as an institution has overshadowed Christian witness by the rank and file church member. He examines Biblical ministry as reflected in the life of our Lord and in the functions of the apostles and first Christians. He recognizes the polarity that has developed between those holding positions "above the people" and the members of the parish. The New Testament however always pictures the church as the *community* of *all* believers in Christ.

Every believer has immediate access to God. No go-between is needed. By deeds, perhaps more than by words, the people make the church present where they are, provided they have a live consciousness of being *in Christ* and have not handed over their God-given priest-

ly functions to officiants of the church. The individual
Christian has immediate access to God which no ecclesiastical authority can destroy or take away.[16]

In his first chapter the author describes the Christian
community with three terms. (1) *Liberty*—Christians
are liberated by Christ *from* the letter of the law, the
burden of guilt, the dread of death. They are at the
same time however liberated *for* life, service and love.
(2) *Equality*—All members of the church have the
same rights and the same duties. "No one in the church
has a right to abolish this fundamental equality of the
faithful." (3) *Fraternity*—The church is a community
of brothers and sisters. They have one Father, our Lord
and Master. They also have one message and one mission—directed to all mankind. This brotherhood must
be made concrete in the *community!*[17]

The personal terms, similes, modes of operation
which Jesus exemplified in His earthly ministry, and the
openness and joint witness, empathy, and fellowship of
the early Christians are the models for our own day.
The letters of St. Paul richly illustrate the fellowship
and witness of the early Christians. They reflect a pluri-
formity, mobility, and flexibility of the ministry in the
varied uses of the Spirit-given charisms in everyday living. Working together in Christian love pervades all of
Paul's letters.

Dr. Küng asserts that the New Testament does not
really speak of a "church office." Instead it focuses on
the term *diakonia,* meaning service to one another by
all members. This is the most typical expression of mission and ministry. With other theologians he maintains
that the New Testament does not establish fixed offices.
It uses a variety of terms and at times interchangeably.
The office of "clergy" is not institutionalized. Apostolic succession cannot be established on theological-
dogmatical grounds. Church structures must remain
open to all possibilities existing in the churches of the

New Testament record. The New Testament, says Küng, gives us *several models* and does not allow us to "canonize one congregational structure alone." The author then shows how the church office of priest-minister was developed into a "priest-craft" from the second century on, which was a departure from the Corinthian model.[18]

WHAT IS "MINISTRY"?

New Testament ministry is capsuled by Küng with five sentences:

(1) The church is above all else "the people of God," a community of believers.

(2) Ministry is mutual service.

(3) The priesthood of all believers is clearly the New Testament pattern.

(4) The church is nurtured by means of the Word and the sharing of charismatic gifts.

(5) Everywhere it is the local church that is to be recognized.[19]

Throughout the book he demonstrates that "ministry" has too long been identified with clergy-status. "Church leadership was never intended to be autocratic leadership" but instead "a coordinating, integrating ministry" to congregation and community. Every Christian is called to a ministry that flows directly from the Gospel. Whoever has the Gospel has also a ministry. Every historian will recognize that this was the teaching of the Protestant reformers.

What then is the pastor's role? He is a member and leader of the Christian community. In a democratized society such as we have in our age, he can be authoritative but not authoritarian. He will serve as inspirer, moderator, animator of the congregation. He will discover and liberate the hidden talents and energies of his people. He will inspire confidence and arouse enthusiasm. He will not simply issue orders. He will not be an "answer man." He will make Jesus Christ LORD always. "In his dedication to Christ he becomes transparent" is the way Küng says it.[20]

The author states that he undertook this study and wrote the book "to prevent anyone from ever again beginning an essay on church ministry by discussing an office intead of the church and from readily presuming as self-evident what is to be said about the community of believers."[21] He says the universal priesthood of all believers rests solidly on Old and New Testament authority. He suggests that the term "priest" should be dropped as a term restricted exclusively to the clergy.[22]

The New Testament gives us various models but establishes no one-and-only fixed form. All believers share in the priesthood of Christ and all are set apart from the world by faith and baptism to fulfill that ministry.[23] Pastors are needed to feed the church of God and to liberate, develop, and utilize the talents and energies of all of God's people. The church must forever gather the people to be built up by the Word and then scatter the people into secular, everyday life to proclaim and live the Word.[24]

Protestant churches should be deeply grateful for this book by Dr. Küng, as well as for Vatican II statements and commentaries on "The Apostolate of the Laity." All Christendom for some decades has in one form or another displayed a new awareness of its mission and ministry *in all sectors of society, in all walks of life, and by all of its people.*

THE NEXT GENERATION

In the Olympics the torch is the symbol of passing on an honored tradition from one Olympiad to another. In the church the concept of the priesthood of believers must likewise be passed on from generation to generation.

Pastors need to ask themselves: How can we effectively teach this central fact of the great commission to every group of new members. Has our parish lost this Christian heritage? Did it ever really possess it? Does our present cooperative ministry of pastor and people reflect it? If so, how clearly? In what degree? What self-image do the people of the parish have of their mission? Is this priestly concept of the believers clearly alive in the *personal* theology of our members? If a true-false type of survey were taken of all youth and adult members, what percentage would report that they understand and practice this priesthood? How well is it being taught at all age levels in the church school? Is it part of our pre-membership training course? Is it taught and caught by *practical* assignments? Or is it merely a mental concept, a mere metaphor already fading away as insignificant? Does the pulpit program each year adequately cover this vital area? Does the operation of the pastorate in your church and the administration of your parish boards and committees, the work of your teachers and elders clearly reflect and embody the practice of this priesthood? *A single minister's pastorate at any one place can lose or can retrieve the "torch of the ministry of all God's people."*

THE SEMINARY'S ROLE

The denominational seminary has an equally strategic role. It can almost exclusively reflect the one-man ministry pastorate or it can teach the stance of the minister as strategist for an inreach into the congregation and for an outreach by all the people of the parish to the whole community. What image is the seminarian getting? Will the graduates develop a new generation of American Christians who carry forward a *people's ministry* as illustrated for us in the Book of Acts?

Seminaries have a strategic task. The priesthood of believers can be lost by a single generation of pastors who think they alone are the priests of the parish. When a pastor is installed in a parish, a true or false image of ministry can be left with the installation rites. What image will you be leaving, Pastor Smith, as you move to another parish?

If Dr. Eastwood were to prepare a new edition of his book for the year 2,000, would he have to repeat the observation: "The priesthood of all believers has never been entirely lost nor has it ever been fully received"?

Chapter
Six

THE LAITY
AND THE CHURCH

WHO IS A LAYMAN?

In today's parlance the term "layman" is generally applied to the person who is a nonprofessional. That means a person who is not "at home" in a certain field of knowledge, whether that be chemistry, botany, teaching, or theology.

It is most often used in regard to personnel in the church. The opposite of layman is clergyman. This usually means the minister of a parish. This current use goes back in history to the appointment of priests by bishops and originated in the post-apostolic life of the church. The term "pastor" means shepherd and the flock he cares for are the laity.

The average layman admires and respects the clergyman and usually thinks that to be a real "minister" he must join the ranks of the clergy. To be sure, pastors are to be honored because they are our spiritual leaders (1 Timothy 5:17). But Christian service is as sacred when performed by a layman as when performed by a seminary graduate or a properly called pastor of a parish.

Laymen are filling significant roles in the church. Buildings must be maintained, the necessary funds must be gathered, rightly expended, and accounted for. Having a keen eye for evaluating the church's budget is important. Christian businessmen have made outstanding contributions to church boards on parish, district, and denomination-wide levels. Millions of churchmen and women are engaged in Sunday and weekday church school structures as teachers and administrators, or they are participating in youth, men's, women's, and couples' groups and giving a variety of parish and community services.

Nevertheless in most churches the laity belongs chiefly to the audience and is engaged in what we call church housekeeping tasks. Unfortunately the layman's own congregation may have given him this limited image of himself.

Unless the average church member has a sense of being called for a mission where he is every day of his life, he has too low an estimate of himself. He may leave most of his mission to the pastor. Or to put it another way, when he goes to his daily work, he may "hang up his Christianity in the cloakroom."

The apostle Paul in the closing chapter of his Letter to the Colossians gives us another picture of the layman. "Masters, treat your slaves justly and fairly" (4:1). "Continue steadfastly in prayer" (v.2). "Conduct yourselves wisely toward outsiders" (v. 5). "Tychicus will tell you about my affairs; he is a beloved brother and faithful *minister* and *fellow servant* in the Lord" (v.7). "With him is Onesimus, the faithful and beloved brother, who is one of yourselves" (v.9). Aristarchus, his fellow prisioner; Mark (very likely the writer of the second Gospel); Joshua, also called Justus, "have been a comfort to me" (vv. 10-11). They were Paul's *"fellow workers* for the kingdom of God" (v. 11). "Epaphras, who is one of yourselves, a *servant* of Christ Jesus, greets you, always remembering you earnestly in his prayers that you may stand mature and fully assured in all the will of God" (v.12). "He has *worked* hard for you and for those in Laodicea" (v.13). "Luke, the beloved physician, [the writer of the third Gospel account] the Demas greet you" (v.14). "Say to Archippus, 'See that you *fulfill the ministry which you have received* in the Lord' " (v.17). At this time there was *no* pastoral office as we know it today!

To the Corinthians Paul wrote, "You are not your own. You were bought with a price. So glorify God *in your body"* (1 Corinthians 6:19-20). In his Second Letter to the Corinthians he says: "You are my *letters of recommendation"* (3:2-3). Paul counted on all his converts as *co-workers.* Peter capsules it well for us: *"Each one* as a good manager of God's different gifts, must use for the good of others the special gift he has received from God" (1 Peter 4:10 TEV).

The individual Christian has a mission no one else can perform for him. It is *untransferable!*

KLEROS AND LAOS ARE THE SAME PEOPLE

One senses at once a closeness between the apostle Paul and the people of the churches which he always considered co-workers. In the post-apostolic period a gulf developed between clergy and laity. This has often been difficult to bridge. Even today many church members feel a distance between themselves and their minister. Titles, formalities, traditions, even the clergy collar, often hinder free communication. However, it would be quite unfair not to acknowledge the warmth and love of parishioners for their pastor, and the pastor for his people. In fact, many pastors have taken the initiative in opening new channels of communication, such

as open forums, consultations, and various types of conferences. Many pastors feel the need for dialog. They
desire two-way communication. Nevertheless some pastors feel an unhappy loneliness due to the gap between
clergy and laity.

To get a solid base for our conversations, it is helpful
to trace our distinctions back to their source. In doing
this we get a few surprises. The word "clergy" is derived
from the Greek work *kleros*. It originally meant the object used in drawing lots to choose a person for a position. It is related to the verb "call" and is employed in
the Greek New Testament when referring to the Holy
Spirit calling a person by the Gospel into the Christian
fellowship of the church. We can understand its meaning better if we see how it is used:

> *"Called* to be God's people. . . . When God *called*
> you" (1 Corinthians 1:2,26 TEV); "When He [God]
> *called* you. . . . To which God has *called* you"
> (Ephesians 4:1,4 TEV); "He saved us and *called*
> us to be His own people" (2 Timothy, 1:9 TEV).[1]

In each of these verses some form of the Greek word
"to call" is used. *All Christians* are God's *called* people,
God's "clergy" in the world! Even the Greek word for
the church, *ekklesia,* is derived from the basic term "to
call."

A study of the word "laity" reveals that it is derived
from the Greek word *laos,* which means "people,"
usually God's chosen people, the Christians. Here is a
sample of its use in the Greek New Testament:

> "Taking from among them a *people* [*laos*] to be His
> own" (Acts 15:14 TEV); "But you are the chosen
> race . . . God's own *people* [*laos*]. . . . At one time
> you were not God's people [*laos*], but now you are
> His *people* [laos]" (1 Peter 2:9-10 TEV).

In each of these verses and in many others we find the
Greek word *laos,* which is the root term for the word
"laity."

When we take a close look at the New Testament, we can see that *all Christians are God's laity (laos)* and *all are God's clergy (kleros)*. Any distinction we make between clergy and laity cannot clear the laity from being ministers of the Gospel or from being responsible as God's "clergy." The above is the way seminary professor William Robinson summarizes the situation.[2]

Elton Trueblood helps us translate this discovery into the late 20th century:

> *So far as the Christian faith is concerned the practical handle in our time is lay religion.* If in the average church we should suddenly take seriously the notion that every lay member, man or woman, is really a minister of Christ, we would have something like a revolution in a very short time; it would constitute both the big dose and the required novelty. Suddenly the number of ministers in the average church would jump *from one* to *five hundred*. This is the way to employ valuable but largely wasted human resources."[3]

For a more extended treatment of the use of *kleros* and *laos* in Scripture consult your Bible dictionaries and the books by Hendrick Kraemer, Francis Ayres, and Howard Grimes. For page references see the footnote.[4]

MINISTRY BY THE PEOPLE TO THE PEOPLE

God's call to gather a people for Himself came first to Abraham with the promise that by him all the families of the earth should be blessed (Genesis 12:1-3). That same call was extended to Jacob and his 12 sons, the forebears of the Israel of God. When the Israelites were in bondage to Pharaoh in Egypt, God's call came to Moses to deliver them as the bearers of God's promise (Exodus 6:6-9). Aaron's family was assigned the priestly function in the tabernacle and temple. *But every Israelite belonged to "God's people" and had a mission to fulfill in his own family* (Deuteronomy 6:4-9; 7:6).

When our Lord came to live with men He not only called and trained 12 men but sent out the Seventy, two by two to call people to discipleship (Luke 10:1-2). After giving the great commission to go into all the world to preach the Gospel to all nations (Matthew 28:19-20) Jesus promised the Holy Spirit *to empower ALL believers to be ambassadors for Christ.*

Jesus' own ministry is our greatest object lesson. He did worship in the temple, but chiefly He ministered where the people were: by the sea of Galilee, with fishermen, and at Jacob's well in Samaria. He was always going places—to people's homes, to the market place. His favorite method was opening up conversation with a question or a miracle of healing. Jesus was to be found where the working man made his living. He was a critic of mere form worship and the manmade rules of the scribes and Pharisees. He refused to be drawn into such legalisms like the length of a Sabbath day journey. Instead He called for repentance and faith. He identified with the new wine, not with the old wineskins. He did not sit with the Sanhedrin but with "sinners." In the eyes of the Pharisees He was not very "religious." What He proclaimed was freedom. He said, "If the Son shall make you free, you are free indeed" (John 8:36). Free from sin! Free from false tradition! Free by God's grace alone!

Jesus cultivated a fellowship of faith, a brotherhood of believers. "You have one teacher, Christ, and *you are all brethren*" (Matthew 23:8). True discipleship, said Jesus, is really *servantship!* (Luke 22:25-26). The Son of man came to *serve!* (Mark 10:45).

When we move into the Book of Acts we note that the 120 disciples elected Matthias to replace Judas. The assembly of believers chose seven "laymen" to minister to the needy, one of them was Stephen. In the persecution following Stephen's martyrdom, the 12 apostles temporarily remained in Jerusalem. The *Christians*—we would use the term laity today—"were all scattered throughout the region of Judea and Samaria." "Those who were scattered went about *preaching* the word. "Philip [one of the seven laymen] went down to a city of Samaria, and *proclaimed* to them the Christ" (Acts 7:54-8:8).

At this time a man named Saul was confronted by Christ in a dramatic vision on the road to Damascus and was directed to carry the Gospel to the Gentiles and kings and the sons of Israel (Acts 9:15). In this manner Saul the persecutor became Paul *the man on a mission*. But he did not work alone. The Book of Acts and his letters indicate that he was an enlister and enabler of many men and women in God's mission.

WHAT ABOUT THE PASTORAL OFFICE?

If it has appeared to you that the case for the laity has been weighted, then it should be acknowledged that American churches have given more prominence to the laity than the European churches. Yet also in America there is a strong equation between church and pastor. Often parishioners put it this way: "I belong to Pastor Smith's church," substituting the name of the pastor for the name of the congregation. The wider treatment of *kleros* and *laos* was necessary to get both clergy and laity to a point where they will *take a second look at each other!*

As long ago as 1876 Bishop J. B. Lightfoot, writer of New Testament commentaries, wrote: "The only priests under the Gospel designated as such in the New Testament are the saints, the members of the Christian brotherhood."[5] This statement is generally accepted by New Testament scholars on the basis of such key passages as 1 Peter 2:9-10. This assertion however raises the question: Does not the apostle Paul speak of pastors, teach-

ers, deacons? And did he not send helpers to serve the
new churches?

We think at once of Paul's Letter to Titus in which he
says: "I left you in Crete for you to put in order the
things that still need doing, and to appoint church elders
in every town" (Titus 1:5 TEV). Some qualifications
for being an "elder" then follow: "He must hold firmly
to the message." The Letters to Timothy are also "pastoral" epistles. More specifically, Paul at three other
places designates certain offices, positions, or services to
which qualified persons are to be appointed. It is significant that all of those so-called "positions" are given
within the larger context of a diversity of gifts given by
the Lord to *all* members of a church.

Let us take a closer look at Paul's letter to the Ephe-
sian Christians. Chapter 4 begins with the *calling* of all
Christians in the congregation. Each member has been
given a special gift (v.7). Christ ascended *"to prepare
all God's people for the work of Christian service"*
(v.12). The ascended Lord gave the church leaders:
"some to be apostles, others to be prophets, others to be
evangelists, others to be pastors and teachers" (V.11
TEV).

Again in First Corinthians 12 the apostle has a longer
dissertation on a variety of gifts *to all members of the
church* at Corinth. Here the list differs from the Ephe-
sian listing. "And God has appointed in the church first
apostles, second prophets, third teachers, then workers
of miracles, then healers, administrators, speakers in
various tongues." Open your Bible to 1 Corinthians 12.
Note especially verses 4 to 11 in which the variety of
gifts are said to be distributed by the spirit *to various
members of that church*. In verses 12 to 26 the purpose
of mutual service by many members in the one body,
with gifts from the one Spirit, is described. Note also
that *eight* types of ministries are listed in vv. 27-31.

A third chapter that is significant is Romans 12.

Once more the apostle begins with an appeal to *every Christian* to "offer himself as a living sacrifice to God, dedicated to His service" (Romans 12:1 TEV). In a longer paragraph he speaks about the best use by all members of the church in Rome in different functions for the building up of the congregation. Note especially his expressions: "if *your* gift is to *preach* . . . if it is to *serve* . . . if it is to *teach* . . . if it is to *encourage*" (Romans 12:3-8 TEV).

From this brief survey we may conclude that various leaders (also laymen) were used in the local church, even as this already had been the practice in the Jewish synagogs (see Luke 4:16-21 for an example). These leaders were called by various names according to their functions. Yet no formal set of offices is prescribed! No bishop is appointed to oversee a diocese. Historians agree that no priestly set of positions were in common use until the latter half of the second century of the Christian era. A case in point: The qualifications for "elders" in Titus chapter 1 (vv. 6-9) are almost identical with the terms used for "bishop" (which means pastor) in 1 Timothy 3:1-13.

Alan Richardson's *A Theological Word Book of the Bible* contains a six-page treatment of "minister" and "ministry" by H. J. Carpenter. Here are his findings: "The New Testament is clear that all the various ministerial functions by which the life of the church is maintained and extended are 'gifts' (charismata: grace gifts) of Christ to the church through the presence and operation of the Holy Spirit within it." With reference to 1 Corinthians 12:29 he says: "In spite of the first three items in the list, St. Paul is *not* here enumerating the ecclesiastical *offices,* but is describing the variety of *functions* and kinds of *service* in the one body (vv. 12-27) which all contribute to the corporate life and arise from the diverse operation of the one spirit within it (vv. 4-11)." Romans 12:5-8 and Ephesians 4:7-12 do *not* therefore "give us evidence about the organized ministry of the early church, though they tell us much of the forms of activity (diversity of gifts) in it."[6]

A Presbyterian study of the Christian ministry comes to the conclusion that Paul's listings were suitable for the planting stage of the early church. It then adds, "The blunt fact is that we are given no supernatural polity in Scripture," only some illuminating examples. This report also states, "Thus we find that Calvin, with Luther, places the emphasis upon 'duties,' 'obedience,' 'services,' and 'functions' of the ministerial office rather than 'status,' 'power,' and 'dignity.' "[7]

In another study of the ministry in the New Testament, the author asserts the need of recovering the Christian doctrine of vocation, and that Luther and Calvin made it clear that the difference between layman and priest is not a difference in "vocation" but a difference in "office." These Reformation leaders did not sweep the minister or priest away, but they declared that the vocation of the layman was as deeply religious as that of the priest, in fact, it too was a priestly vocation.[8]

This study does not call into question the office of the pastoral ministry or the practice of ordination. It does deal with the more strategic use of the pastoral office in the deployment of the whole congregation for the fuller exercise of every Christian's God-given priesthood.

The basic conclusion with which scholars agree is the one given by Paul in 1 Corinthians 14:40. After listing many gifts the Spirit has given "for the edification of the whole Church," the apostle writes, "Everything must be done in a proper and orderly way" (vv. 34,40 TEV).

The Committee for Scholarly Research of The Lutheran Church—Missouri Synod in 1963 called together competent historians and theologians to reexamine the Biblical basis for the church's ministry and its application to our time. Their findings were: "Within the confines of the Biblical record itself, the apparatus of offices and tasks is multiform and fluid. All share in a common ministry for edification of the church. The special ones [meaning pastors, etc.] are distinguished from the ministry of all saints in that they are a gift of Christ and of the Spirit to the rest, for the good of all." This study also says, "Justin Martyr (ca. 150) calls the special ministers teachers, lecturers, presidents, deacons. He regards the whole Christian community as the high-priestly race of God. The president was the spokesman of these people in worship and especially in the celebration of the Lord's Supper."[9]

William Dallmann shows the relation between the universal priesthood of all believers and the clergy: "The Old Testament distinction between priest and people, clergymen and laymen, is at an end. Christ, our High Priest, has made all Christians priests before God. All Christians are God's clergy, and there is no special clerical order in the church. The ministry is an office, not an order, much less a threefold order of bishops, priests, and deacons."[10]

In his book, *Why Priests? A Proposal for a New Church Ministry,* Hans Küng comes to the same conclusion, namely, that the New Testament does not really speak of a fixed church office. It uses a variety of terms almost interchangeably. The clergy office is not institutionalized. The New Testament gives us many models. This does not permit us to "canonize" one congregational structure alone.[11]

At this point we need to recognize the office of the pastor in the modern church. His leadership through the centuries has not been accidental or optional. Leadership is necessary in any enterprise, be that in government, business, school, or church. His role in the modern church will become more apparent in the remaining chapters of this book, but the emphasis will be on his role as an enabler, teacher, and shepherd of all his members.

TRANSITION FROM OLD TESTAMENT TO NEW TESTAMENT

We have seen that no fixed forms, organizational structures, or definite ranking of full-time servants in the church can be established from the New Testament Scriptures. Converts from Judaism had a hard time understanding the transition to the New Testament as both the Book of Acts and the Book of Hebrews indicate. It is significant that it was the apostle Peter who in his two letters most explicitly described the ministry of the New Testament as a *priesthood of all believers!*

The establishment of the bishop's office is *not* by divine order. But churches later found it helpful to set up some offices to provide guidance, order, and supervision. The result has been a number of different forms. Both the Greek and the Roman Churches set up a two-level structure, one story for priests and bishops and a lower story for the laity. A trip to your encyclopedia will give you the details and the extent of this two-tier structure.

The 16th century Reformation was the turning point. It opened up the whole question of the laity. The conflict became dramatic when Martin Luther challenged the church with his 95 thesis at Wittenberg and his heroic stand at Worms. Churches have never been the same since! Vast new areas of thought were opened up as the priesthood of all believers was championed.

All divisions of Christendom had to face the larger question: To whom did Christ entrust the keys of the church? To bishops and pastors only, or to the whole *laos*—all the people of God? (Matthew 18:15-20). What is more significant is that the church of whatever doctrinal persuasion in every generation and especially in the phenomenally different world of our present age must reexamine its structure in the light of the ministry of *all* of God's people.

THE PASTORATE IN AMERICA

The opening of the new world was a new challenge. As the colonists came to American shores they brought their religion with them and their concepts of the church. Separation from the continental churches to which they belonged (with their connection to the political state), the challenge of the new American frontier, and identification with a corresponding denomination in the new world raised again such questions as "What is the church?" and "Where is the church?" Most immigrants sought out congregations in their own tradition. It was on American soil that freedom allowed a new look, especially also at the structure of churches.

The old-world forms and structures were usually duplicated in the new world. Government under the Roman pontiff, who appoints American cardinals, continues for people of the Church of Rome. The Episcopal pattern follows the forms of the Anglican Church. The Lutheran and Reformed Churches set up their own synods in America on a confessional basis, with modifications toward complete self-government, instead of ties to a state church as in some European countries. The congregational pattern was adopted by many of the new churches: Congregationalists, Baptists, Disciples of Christ, Lutheran, Pentecostal, and the like.

The church in every age, from the apostolic era to the present, needs to derive both form and direction from its mission. It needs an evangelical, theological basis. It needs farsighted leadership. It needs a structure and polity which will harness its "people power" for world mission. This is to say that *the priesthood of all people must be effectively implemented.*

The real image of the church is not institutional. The church is Christian men and women in dialog with God

*and with each other to equip themselves for evangelical
witness, wherever they are in the world and in all the
structures of life.* The individual Christian needs a congregation of believers who serve each other and are
served by a spiritual leader, the pastor, their enabler
and counselor. Every Christian needs constant renewal
of faith, growth to spiritual manhood, ongoing training
to equip himself or herself for Christ's mission in the
family, in the neighborhood, in his business and profession, in his citizenship and in every station or place
where he or she has contact with another person. *The
Christian is to be Christ's servant in all sectors of life.*

THE CHURCH INSTITUTIONALIZED

From our investigation in this chapter we may draw
two conclusions. Even the churches which are not hierarchical in structure and feel historically and theologi-
cally close to the priesthood of all believers in their doctrinal theology have nevertheless left most of their
priestly tasks up to their pastors. American churches in
the thinking of the average person are often more like
institutions that have to be maintained than broth-
erhoods of people personally at work in mission.

When a Norwegian theologian left America after an
extended visit he was asked: "What did you find the
church in America to be?" He replied, "I found it to be
a pastor's church."[12]

Albert McClellan puts his evaluation tersely: "A
church more concerned about its building, its organization, its size, its budget, and its place among the institutions of the community than it is about its mission, has
lost its dynamic and no longer has a reason for being. It
can regain its vitality only as it visualizes itself according to the many ways the New Testament characterized
the people of God."[13]

A seminary professor of church history writes: "In
spite of its affirmation of the priesthood of all believers,

there is perhaps no function which Protestantism has so much neglected. Not only have Protestant laymen not assumed the priestly role, but until recently even the clergy have shunned it. A major task for Protestant churches today, not merely the clergy, but the whole church, is to understand and accept their priesthood."[14]

Our search for a Biblical image of the church in action has posed a number of vital questions. What image does the average church member have of himself? Does the church exist for its members only or do its members exist to fulfill their mission in life? *How can we change the "consumer only" viewpoint of so many church members?* Where will the initiative for change have to come from? How can we help pastors and people recapture the full meaning and application of 1 Peter, Chapter 2?

Chapter Seven | # THE MINISTRY OF THE LAITY

IN SIX SECTORS OF LIFE

It was the German theologian Christoph Blumhardt the Elder who said, "First the human being must become a Christian. Then the Christian must become a human being. And this second conversion is sometimes missing." Blumhardt wanted to capture the idea that the person, having found Christ, is born again. He has a "new humanity." He is called by God not only to live in the world, but to find his chief field of service there. Being a Christian is not an escape from the world into the church. It is taking the Gospel and its healing ministry out where the people are. Our Lord's description of the last judgment confirms this concept (Matthew 25:31-45).

Recent decades have seen some significant movements by the church to direct the Christian out into the world with a new sense of mission. After World War II the German Kirchentag was such a call to be the church where you are. The evangelical academies, like the one at Bad Boll (Germany), called businessmen, statesmen, tradesmen together to recapture their Christian citizenship and to put it to work in their vocations. "Faith and Life" missions on American college campuses involved laity and clergy to discuss religion in daily life. The emphasis was on "witnessing where you are!"

The Christian faith is not a cloak we put into the coat closet when we come home from church. It is a lively, life-giving thing; it cannot but do the works of God which the Holy Spirit puts into the heart. Faith in Christ is *dynamic*. It cannot be confined to static church membership, as this is commonly understood.

We need to recognize gratefully the women's federations and guilds of all church denominations. They have done great things in missionary education and services and contributed large sums of money for home and foreign mission projects. They have given abundantly of their talents in the auxiliaries of hospitals, institutes for the blind and the deaf, and hundreds of welfare projects. The men of the churches have supported Christian radio and television programs for a worldwide outreach of the Gospel. Today there is a refreshing revival of Christian witness by new youth movements in the church. Important as these joint services are, they must not obscure personal witness by word and deed.

The recovery of the ministry of the laity demands more than voluntary services at the church. It involves the acceptance of one's daily work as an expression of the priesthood of all believers. It includes training for all aspects of discipleship, turning our Christian confessions into a philosophy of life and using our talents wherever we are out there in the world!

A CHRISTIAN SENSE OF VOCATION

Many people today do not know what they are living for. They lack a sense of worth and direction. Recovery begins with finding a challenging life purpose.

Modern man may feel like a cog in a big machine, like the workman who for 8 hours a day runs a stamping machine that produces a part for an airplane engine. But he does not know what its purpose is!

Donald Heiges in his book *The Christian Calling,* tells the story of a gang of laborers drilling holes 5 feet deep in a street. Their boss did not tell them the purpose. In fact, he looked in each hole and then said, "Okay, fill 'er up." At noon the men announced: "We quit. Pay us off." When the boss asked why, they replied, "Digging holes and filling them up only makes fools of us." Then he told them why the drilling was done—to find the location of a "lost" water main. Deep down a human being wants to see some point to what he is doing, even if what he is doing makes no great demands upon the mind or body.[1]

Both the "machine man" and the "organization man" can become depersonalized in our highly mechanized society. A Christian understanding of vocation is tremendously relevant to the problem of meaninglessness in our entire culture. We are living in a sensate culture. It is materialistic to a degree which the common people have perhaps never before experienced. "Man does not live by bread alone," said Jesus. Neither can he really live by sports alone, gourmet eating alone, accumulation of wealth alone, or an endless round of social affairs. Today's man and woman are consumer-conscious and involved in a new grab for more and more things that can leave a man spiritually bankrupt.

Joseph Fort Newton puts man's dilemma most forcefully:

> When a man loses faith in God, he worships humanity; When faith in humanity fails, man worships science; When faith in science fails, he worships himself; Hence the tedious egotism of our day, when men are self-centered and self-obsessed, unable to get themselves out of their own hands.[2]

Man must have a reason and a goal for living. Life must have a vertical dimension as well as a horizontal dimension. For this he needs insights, guides, and purposes which go beyond mere existence. In other words, he needs a sense of vocation. The mission Christ left for His followers gives him that calling.

Israel had such a sense of mission, a destiny beyond mere living. God wrote His purpose upon their hearts (Jeremiah 31:31-33).

Christians have an even greater self-understanding and reason to serve God and their fellowmen. We are God's offspring! (Acts 17:26-28). We are more than part of the human race. We are the people of the fulfillment. In us the ministry of Christ to all people is to continue (Acts 2:39; 3:25). God has "called us with a holy calling, not in virtue of our own works but *in virtue of His own purpose* and the grace which He gave us in Christ Jesus" (2 Timothy 1:9).

In 1 Corinthians 7 the apostle Paul emphasizes faithful stewardship in our earthly profession (vv. 17,20,24). Applied today, it means honest and responsible service on our jobs, whatever they may be. By our manner of life the people around us are to discover the inner drive God gives us. They are to recognize us by the way we work. The apostle Paul put it this way in 1 Corinthians 9:19-23 TEV: "I make myself everybody's

slave in order to win as many as possible. . . . I become
all things to all men, that I may save some of them by
any means possible."

This is the secret of the Christian's vocation. This is
the way Donald Heiges puts it: "When the flame of
faith burns brightly and the Spirit breaks through the
crust of routine experience, then his vocation takes
wings and each moment is transfigured with joy."[3]

After World War II a group of educators were dealing with a skeletal program for the postwar reconstruction period. At the end of their statement of aims they
made the following significant assertion:

> To embody these principles into the society of the fu-
> ture, men must be inspired by forces which spring
> from a deeper dimension of life. This has often been
> overlooked or forgotten in recent generations, and
> this is the crisis of our civilization! To develop men
> need action; to act men need faith; to keep the faith
> men need a vision of excellence; and all this is empty
> unless it is pervaded by love and love is action![4]

Being a Christian in the innumerable places where you
are in the course of your entire life span—that is your
Christian vocation.

WOMEN AND MEN IN THE PUBLIC DOMAIN

The churches have in the past left the impression that
the Lord has entrusted His commission mainly to men.
Both women and men are included in the "people of
God" concept. In today's society women have equality
with men in citizenship, education and vocation. Wom-
en's roles have greatly increased and become very di-
versified. Women are practically in every major profession in increased numbers, and this is so in almost all
parts of the world. In American society woman is closer
to the community than man. The family is one place
where the greatest impact is still made and will be made

by the wife and mother. Woman's roles have increased tremendously in all areas of our society.

We need to ask: Are both Christian men and women as active in the public domain as they should be? Social justice is taught in many places in the Scriptures. Do we "operationalize" God's demands for a just society? Have we forgotten the prophets of old? Have we limited the term "calling" to the idealized spiritual realm and by-passed the social area? God's people are especially called to become beacons in the world in which they live. They are still part of God's creation called to express Christian convictions and basic human concerns wherever they are. We have a responsible trusteeship for the physical, social, political worlds in which we live. It is possible nevertheless to crawl back into a mental-spiritual realm and bypass the outward expression of the righteousness taught by Christ.

This area is basic in understanding and implementing the term "Christian vocation."

VOCATIONAL COUNSELING

Having defined vocation, we proceed to the question: Who is giving our rising generation vocational guidance with this Christian philosophy? It is precisely here that the Christian congregation through its pastor, teachers, parents, youth leaders has a particularly vital role to play, using its workers as career counselors to high school and college youth. Is your teaching personnel close enough to your youth to give this kind of assistance? Does your parish library have tracts, college bulletins, and books on careers available for youth classes and groups? Every person needs to be given "a vision of excellence." This guidance should be carefully planned with youth. Career counseling may include such items as:

(1) Discovering a person's talents and potentials;

(2) Getting a Christian concept of the place and purpose of work;

(3) Determining how a career becomes a Christian vocation;

(4) Looking at the needs of civilization in our times;

(5) When is leadership Christian? in business, government, education, law, medicine, social work, etc.

Many approaches may be used; for instance, inviting career men and women to describe their jobs and how they work in them as Christians. Ask high school and college teachers to speak to your youth (once a year) to give guidance from actual counseling experience.

Donald Heiges shows how vital a Christian sense of calling is for building a Christian life. "This is the key to the meaning of history and to the meaning of human existence itself. The call of God is both a wondrous and an awesome thing. To be called is to come face to face with great promise and with great peril. To respond in trust and obedience is possible only by the grace of Him who calls."[5]

Every worship service and teaching facility of the parish can become a training center for Christian vocation. However, if the church continually *inspires* but does *not equip for service* it fails its chief Commissioner, the Lord Jesus Christ. If the impression has been given that holiness is being cloistered with God, then it needs to be unlearned!

SIX SECTORS OF SERVICE

When God calls a person through the Gospel, He calls the whole person and lays claim to his whole life. Martin Luther's way of looking at the wholeness of life led him to speak of two realms in which the believer lives: the kingdom of grace and the political kingdom. Both are God's kingdoms, he said, for life cannot be separated into two neat categories: sacred and secular.

This very concept divides a person's loyalties, breaks up his philosophy of life, and makes him a split-personality. It is this wide sweep that is involved in total surrender to Christ (Romans 12:1; 1 Corinthians 10:31). This is the Christian ethic.[6]

"Love born of faith and the Spirit effects a complete breakthrough of the boundary between the two kingdoms," says Gustav Wingren; "the task of the church includes a continuing renewal of the worldly orders, a never-ending alertness in all vocations, from princely to the meanest labor."[7]

Having established a basis for Christian vocation, we may get a broader view of the laity at work if we think of six major areas:

(1) *The Personal Sector*. Being a Christian means having a personal relationship with God through Christ. This becomes central in our way of thinking, in selecting our purpose in life, in our pursuit of personal goals, in our relation to other persons. This relationship is expressed in our practice of prayer, our personal use of the Bible, our expressions of faith in and outside the Christian fellowship and in our words and deeds. It is reflected in our whole philosophy of life!

(2) *The Family Sector*. The Christian faith comes to expression in many ways in the closest of all relationships: between husband and wife, parents and children, brothers and sisters. Words and acts of Christian love, helpfulness and kindness are the media by which we express our calling by God to serve each other. As loyal followers of our Lord we fulfill our roles as teachers, devotional leaders, counselors, and enablers. We help our children choose Christian life-goals. We give the home a Christian atmosphere. Reli-

gion is caught as well as taught; and most effectively in the home.

(3) *The Congregational sector.* The church is our
alma mater (nourishing mother). We express
our identity with "the people of God of all ages"
in common worship, in expressions of fellowship, in accepting the commission Christ gives
to all of His followers, in our local parish.
There, in the congregation, we have our faith
built up, are trained for witness, cooperate in
worldwide ministry and mission activities. No
man is an island. No Christian can long remain
attached to the body of Christ if he personally
lacks a realistic contact with that body. It is here
that we participate personally in learning, teaching, visiting, working, serving, supporting, witnessing. Over the span of the Christian life we
both receive and give in the local church. Christian men, women, youth, and children have a
"churchly vocation."

(4) *The Community Sector.* The congregation's
physical facilities do not exist solely for the congregation's use. They are to serve the whole
community, and in various ways. Each member,
whether on the evangelism committee or not,
has a calling to the people who live next door,
down the street, in the immediate neighborhood,
as well as in the slums or in a new housing development. The care for the poor, the disadvan-
taged, the sick belongs to every Christian's mission as our Lord's account in Matthew 25 so
graphically portrays. The terms Jesus used for
the mission and ministry of all of God's people
imply community services of various kinds. We
are to be the light, leaven, salt of the earth.
Every parish is to be a social service center as
well as an evangelistic center.

(5) *The Occupational Sector.* The Christian is to be "visible" every day on his job. He can hide his faith or he can express his faith by his manner of conversation, the language he uses, the spirit in which he does his work, the fairness and considerateness he expresses to his fellow workmen and his boss. The entire industrial-commercial complex of modern civilization is an area of concern for the Christian citizen. He witnesses on his job by what he says, by how he works, by his honest workmanship, and by his concern for his fellow workers. Every Christian, whether employer or employee, board member or manager, day laborer or technician, office worker or professional (physician, lawyer, teacher) is in a sense to be an *on-the-job worker-priest!*

(6) *The Civic–Political Sector.* The Christian person's vocation involves his civic mindedness, his interest in human rights and equal employment opportunities, and his readiness to serve in public offices for which he is qualified. He is concerned for every aspect of good government and sound legislation. He keeps himself informed on community, city, state, and national affairs. He should be concerned about the Universal Declaration of Human Rights and their application or practice throughout the world. Christian women as well as men should become advocates of good government and be well-informed citizens. They must not stand idly by while justice is defeated and crime increases.[8]

Christian vocation is a vital segment of the individual Christian's ministry of the laity. Is your parish working only in the personal and congregational sectors? Who is responsible for the priesthood in the family sector? Does every parish need a specific and realistic program of ministry to all its families? How effective is your community evangelism work? Is it confined to an occasional crusade or is it ongoing? How do your people score in the occupational and the civic-political sectors? Are they vitally concerned with social justice in the community in which they live? Does your town or city reflect a Christian ethos because the Christians in your community are articulate? All six of these areas belong to the ministry of the laity in a very special way, *because it is the laity that is daily "out there where the action is."*

CHURCH MEMBERSHIP AND DISCIPLESHIP

You will not find the words "church member" in a Bible concordance, but you will frequently encounter the word "disciple." It is the term used to designate believers in Christ over 260 times in the four Gospels and the Book of Acts. Too often when we read these books and come to the word "disciple" we think of the 12 apostles. One observer says it is used of the Twelve fewer than 30 times.

The term "Christian" came into use much later. In the Bible it is found in only three verses: Acts 11:26; 26:28; 1 Peter 4:16.

Jesus went into the villages and made *disciples—followers, learners, witnesses.* He did not enroll people in the local synagogue. He introduced a new and grander concept: membership in the kingdom of God. He did this, chiefly, not in the corridors of the temple or in the synagog, but in the narrow streets of towns in Judea, Samaria, and Galilee and on the highways between these towns. He entered into conversation with people. He awakened their interest with parables. He healed the sick. He performed a miracle at a wedding. He interrupted a funeral procession and restored a young man to life. He spoke to a tax collector and invited Himself into his home. He went to the sea and enlisted fishermen. He said to them: "Repent and believe. Become

My disciples. Learn of Me. As My Father has sent Me, so I now send you." The Christian's main work is out in the world where he is to make contact with all sorts of people and invite them to become disciples.

Jesus gave the Twelve the great commission. Then He ascended into heaven leaving the Holy Spirit to work among them. The Book of Acts shows how active the first Christians were (Acts 8:1-8).

Writing about the church in the 1970s, Albert Mc-Clellan says: "The despair is that the church has not really captured all of its sons and daughters. It has been more concerned with church rolls than with Christian experience. Its emphasis has been more on belonging than understanding. It has built its program more on established forms than on its actual purpose. The church has not asked: 'What am I for? What is my source of power?' "[9]

When the discipleship concept gets blurred in the churches and the priesthood of believers is not even recognized, much less understood, congregations become more interested in themselves than in the fellowship, mission, and service Jesus assigned to them. Here are some portraits of the church that do *not* come up to the Biblical blueprint.

> At times the churches have regarded themselves as Noah's ark of salvation, fortified camps, God's minorities, spiritual fellowships, ecclesiastical societies, temples where God lives, family clubs, and in many other ways. These half-true notions grow out of the experience of Christians in their environment. Most of these concepts are based on an understanding of the church as a place to go to or an organization to belong to. These are "come structures" in contrast with "go structures."[10]

At this point we need to make a confession, and David Schuller puts it into words: "We need to repent.

We have loved our comfort more than we have loved our God. We have loved our churches and our organizations to the point of idolatry. We have spoken of humility while pride of accomplishment swells within our breasts."[11]

The recovery of a ministry of the laity will take place as more church-members think of themselves as *disciples*, ever learning and growing; and *disciplers*, leading non-Christians into the fellowship of believers.

A THEOLOGY OF THE LAITY

Fortunately we have learned to use the term "theology" for more than a system of doctrines to be believed. The whole character, nature, and essence of the Bible teaches an involvement of all of God's people in the mission God gave us. More and more Christian leaders are asking, "What is an adequate ministry?"

An adequate ministry is not a one-man ministry. It is not even a corps of associate pastors. It is the whole church, congregation by congregation, mobilized and trained for mission. Only this strategy is adequate. In his book *Resurgence of the Gospel* T. A. Kantonen observes that the Reformation recovered both the doctrine of justification by faith and the priesthood of all believers; and that "only the two together could give the Gospel to the whole world."[12]

Martin Luther put this role of the laity in down-to-earth terms: "The idea that the service to God should have to do only with a church, altar, singing, reading, sacrifice, and the like is without a doubt but the worst trick of the devil. How could the devil have led us more effectively astray than by the narrow conception that service to God takes place only in church and by works done therein. . . . The whole world could abound with services to the Lord, *Gottesdienste*—not only in churches but also in the home, kitchen, workshop, field."[13]

Under the arresting title *The Tragedy of the Unem-*

ployed, Richard C. Halverson wrote: "Paralleling the misconception of the work of the church is a corresponding notion that the real influence of the church in the world is institutional. . . . Neither the influence of council or clergy, nor the influence of Church boards or administrators, is her power index. . . . God's method is men, not machinery. . . . They are there every day, quietly invading their worlds for Christ, beachheads of the kingdom, in business, education, government, labor, and the professions established by regenerate men doing their job daily to the glory of God as servants of Jesus Christ. This is the work of the church."[4]

Hendrik Kraemer has given us the basic book in his *A Theology of the Laity.* He observes that only occasionally has the ministry of the laity been recognized as an integral and essential part of the functioning of the church. Lay people, and they alone, in their daily lives and occupations encounter the society in which they live. They form in a very particular way the spearhead of the church's true mission. The church exists primarily not to increase its membership but to bring men and women to Christ.

Kraemer speaks of the only partially used members of congregations as "the frozen assets of the church." He suggests a new self-understanding within the church as a "Christocratic fraternity" with a larger role for the laity in the worship services, the teaching functions, the witnessing functions, and greater use of working groups and individuals interpenetrating the world and in this way communicating to it. The church needs to be a gathered fellowship for worship, instruction, and training for the very purpose of being dispersed into society.

"The reformers re-evaluated the common life and *Christian 'vocation'* in the light of the New Testament and found no warrant for dividing life and work into the 'religious' and the 'secular.' The Protestant Christian is to 'be the church' in the area of his daily work and life and to be the church *in the home*. Any useful, honest work, done under responsibility to God, is quite on a par with the ministry or with so-called 'religious' work. There is only one vocation or calling, and that is 'discipleship' in the situation where we live; it is, in Luther's words, to be a Christ to one's neighbor."[15]

"Most lay people," says Kraemer, "are quite satisfied with the contributory place accorded them, because they have never thought about their true place, nor have ever been encouraged to think in that line. Nearly all expositions on the church are magnetically attracted to the treatment of the place and function of the ordained ministry, whereas the laity as the complementary part either remains out of sight or the view of the church becomes too laicized. The treatment of the place and function of the ordained ministry is quite in order, because they have indeed their own important place and function; but the reticence of the laity shows the one-sidedness."[16]

The recovery of the ministry of the laity can come only as the church revises its structure by training its people not to be institutional maintenance men and women but God's messengers in everyday life.[17]

WANTED:
A FUNCTIONAL MINISTRY

CHURCHES THAT SHOW US HOW

The church is all of God's people in ministry sharing the Gospel with people of all nations. The church is more than a place for a certain ritual for worship. It is especially not an institution. The church is reborn flesh-and-blood people who are God's agents of reconciliation (2 Corinthians 5:17-21). The church is a living organism.

All of God's people belong to the New Testament "ministerium." The word "minister" is usually equated with "clergy." It is *not* so in the Bible. In Scripture it is closely linked to the Greek word *diakonia*. This may be translated "service" or "ministry." And it is by no means restricted to what a pastor does in a church building.

SIX TYPES OF NEW TESTAMENT MINISTRY

In the past theologians and historians have defined "ministry" in the light of the organized church's use of the term in the post-apostolic period. To get a solid basis, "ministry" needs to be defined as it is used in the New Testament. The tasks of the minister in a parish include preaching, leading worship services, administering the sacraments, officiating at weddings and funerals, visiting the sick, giving leadership to the church council and in fact to the entire operation of a parish.

Today's Bible scholars are determining the essence of ministry inductively, that is, from the usage of a number of terms in their Biblical context. We shall take a closer look to get a better understanding of "ministry." We first note that Scripture speaks of *ministers* (plural).

We shall look at the Greek terms used in the New Testament (Anglicized for English readers) and give a few references where the Greek term is employed. This does not always show up in the English translation. Use of several English translations will help. Students of Greek can go directly to the Greek New Testament.

(1) **Ministry Through Proclamation.** The apostles went forth "preaching." They proclaimed the good news of prophecy fulfilled in the teaching, life, suffering, death, and resurrection of Jesus Christ. But this preaching was not restricted to the 12 apostles. It was done by all the converts. "The *believers* who were scattered abroad went everywhere preaching the message" (Acts 8:4 TEV). Preaching was not confined to one place or done only by one select person. It was telling both individuals and assembled groups the good news that Christ Jesus had set men free. This was done by any Christian, anytime, anywhere. The original Greek term and English equivalent are given. Note also how often "teaching" and "preaching" are used in the same sentence:

To proclaim as a herald, *kerysso* (verb), *kerygma* (noun) Matthew 4:17, 23; Acts 8:5; 1 Corinthians 9:16.

To announce good news, *euaggelizo* (verb), *euaggelion* (noun) Luke 9:6 TEV; Romans 1:15,16; 1 Corinthians 9:16.

(2) **Ministry Through Teaching.** Jesus went about teaching: in the temple, in the synagog, on His journeys up and down Judea, Samaria, and Galilee. Jesus did more teaching than preaching. This is clear from the four Gospel records. He was a master at getting people to talk. His teaching was conversational and sometimes

controversial. He began with the situation in hand. A cursory reading of the Gospel of John will show how much and how effectively He taught—usually in dialog form. We have much to learn from His method. Two terms are used chiefly to describe this kind of ministry:

To teach: *didasko* (verb), *didache* (noun) Matthew 28:20; Acts 5:42; 15:35; 18:25.

To make disciples: *matheteuo* (verb) *mathethes* (noun) Matthew 28:19; Mark 7:17; Acts 14:21.

(3) **Ministry Through Worship.** Gathering with other Christians for hearing the Gospel, for prayer, praise, and recommitment, which we call a worship-service. The Germans call it *Gottesdienst*—service to God! It is also a service of support and fellowship for our fellow Christians. The singing of Christian hymns is as much a confession of faith as the recital of the Apostles' Creed. It is here that the *laos* (people of God) becomes visible. Fortunately pastors are making worship services less formal and more participative. This is done by the use of fresh, modern-day language in our responses and prayers. We also have folk services with the laity reading the Scripture lesson, singing contemporary hymns, reading from new translations of the Bible, expressing fellowship by having the worshipers pass the bread and cup to each other.

In addition to public worship, the Christian worships in personal, table, and family devotions. Sunday worship should set the stage for the worshipful life (Romans 12:1). We have adapted the term "liturgy" from a Greek term *leitourgia,* now used for various orders of worship services. Old Testament worship by the priest for the people is referred to by the word *latreia* in the New Testament. More closely related to our understanding of worship are:

To pay homage to: *proskyneo* (verb), *proskynetes* (worshiper) John 4:20-24; 1 Corinthians 14:25.

To worship publicly: *latreuo* (verb), *latreia* (service to God) Philippians 3:3; Hebrews 9:1.

One of the fullest expressions of worship is found in Colossians 3:12-17. Note the many terms used: compassion, kindness, patience, forbearance, forgiving, loving, admonishing, singing, thanking.

(4) **Ministry of Fellowship.** Fellowship in the Christian sense has two dimensions: upward to God and outward toward man. The Holy Spirit, who gives us repentance and faith, supplies the vertical dimension, our relation to God. He also by a common faith unites all believers in the communion of saints. This gives fellowship its horizontal dimension. The cement which ties believers of all races together is a common faith in Christ and selfgiving love. First Corinthians 13 uses the uniquely Christian term *agape* for love. With this gift of love a new sense of fellowship is given. Of the 3,000 converts on Pentecost it is said: "They spent their time in learning from the apostles, taking part in fellowship, and sharing in the fellowship meals and prayers" (Acts 2:42 TEV). Two Greek words help us identify and express this fellowship:

Fellowship, have communion with: *koinonia* (noun), Acts 2:41,42; Philippians 1:5; as partnership, 1 John 1:3,7.

Love, affection for: *agape* (noun), 1 Corinthians 13:1-4,8; John 13:34,35; Romans 13:8-10.

(5) **Ministry of Witness.** Every Christian convert is called to be a missionary wherever he is stationed in life. He is to testify to the meaning of the Gospel in his own life. We are to testify verbally and to exhibit visually that we are followers of Jesus Christ, doing this by what we are, by how we live, by the goals in our lives. We have already referred to public proclamation. Announcing the Good News is not restricted to the ordained minister. It is the layman's first duty. We are all to be evangelists, each of us in our own way; each of us using

our own pulpit: a desk at the office, a seat beside the neighbor in the bus or on an airplane; our workbench at the factory, our chair in the lunchroom, our car as we drive a neighbor to the hospital.

The Greek word for witness is *martyria* from which we have derived the English word "martyr." Stephen was one of the first Christians who gave his life as a witness to his faith (Acts 7:58). Every Christian is called to bear witness to his faith. Yet we are often too fearful to give a clear testimony. Kenneth Cober reminds us that Christians are called to testify wherever they are.

Too often the church insulates itself from the world. It withdraws into the haven of the organized church work, in a quest for peace of mind, and escapes the rugged responsibilities of witnessing to the world. Too often do we identify the work of the church with holy places, sacred times, and pious meetings. We frequently conceal our proclamation in a confusing jargon. This is just the reverse of what Jesus commanded. We are to be salt, light, yeast.[1]

> Testimony, *martyrion* (noun) or its verb form are found in: Matthew 24:14; John 1:7,8,15; Acts 1:8; 2:32; 5:32; 26:16.

(6) **Ministry of Service.** The Greek term for service is *diakonia,* from which the English words "deacon" and "deaconess" are derived. Full-time modern deaconesses and deacons were first trained in Europe in the early 19th century. The church speaks of their work as "diaconic services." A helpful stream of such workers is being prepared to serve in a variety of fields: teaching, nursing, care of the aged, service to the handicapped, ministry to the poor, services to families, and workers in home and foreign mission fields. Equally given to Christian services are the thousands of "brothers" and "sisters" of Roman Catholic orders. But *diakonia* is not restricted to or assigned only to full-time workers in the New Testament. Jesus came "teaching, preaching, heal-

ing." All Christians are to gird themselves for service as Jesus did in the footwashing of the Upper Room. "I have given you an example," He said! Jesus drives home the importance of such ministry in His unforgettable words, "What you have done to the least of these My brethren you have done unto Me." (Matthew 25). Christians are called to be servants!

Service to others: *diakonos* (servant), *diakonia* (service) Matthew 20:26,28; Mark 10:43-45.

Servant (*doulos* is also used for slave) Matthew 20:28; Galatians 5:13; Philippians 1:1.

In verb form: Romans 1:1; 6:22.

The general impression we get from this brief survey of terms is that *the congregation is to be a brotherhood of ministers led by and fed by the congregational shepherd.* These six functions of the New Testament priesthood involve all believers: a congregation of three, or three hundred; or a church body of 3 million or 9 million. This sixfold ministry is given to all persons by the Holy Spirit to proclaim, teach, worship, love, witness, and serve.[2]

THE IMPORTANCE OF MINISTRY IN FAMILIES

Closely related to the teaching function are the many New Testament references to nurture in the family. There are at least four references in the New Testament to "the church in your house" (Romans 16:5; 1 Corinthians 16:19; Colossians 4:15; Philemon 2). Commentators usually consider this phrase as a reference to worship services conducted in the homes of believers during the period when they are no longer permitted to gather in synagogues and had not yet built their own edifices for Christian worship. Gathered in homes, the first Christians taught the Word, confessed the faith, and shared their witness.

The Old Testament Passover was celebrated in homes. To all Israel God said: "These words which I command you this day shall be upon your heart; and you shall teach them diligently to your children, and shall talk of them when you sit in your house, and when you walk by the way, and when you lie down, and when you rise" (Deuteronomy 6:6-7). The apostolic letters give similar directions (Ephesians 5:21 to 6:4; Colossians 3:12-25; 1 Peter 3:1-7). They extend to all times and places. Educators and historians agree that the home, not only the church and the school, holds the key to developing the Christian's personality and his habits of life. The family provides the climate, the atmosphere, the philosophy of life, the value systems, the habit patterns of people. This does not deny the role of schools and other character-forming agencies. It simply asserts the psychological experience of the human race. With the moral decline of our age, Christian teaching and example in the family do not become less important but more important!

This has major implications for the church. The tendency has been, and still is, for parents to shift their religious responsibilities to outside teaching agencies including the church. Parents need to learn what the church is teaching. And more important, the church needs to learn what the parents are teaching—or not teaching. It is quite possible that the theology of the home is canceling out the theology of the church. *Both teachers and parents are likely to put too much trust in learning formulas and facts and too little trust in situational learning—verbal and nonverbal.* Unfortunately even Christian parent-teacher meetings are more school-oriented or church-oriented than they are parent or family oriented.

For the church's ministry this means: (1) involving parents in Christian nurture (from birth on), (2) upgrading the status of parents, (3) helping families develop a Christian life-style, (4) affirming and implementing the church's ministry to the whole family, and (5) enlisting the family in the "lay ministries" outlined earlier in this chapter.

What does this imply for the pastoral care of families? What does it require of the educational philosophy and practical operation of the church's teaching agencies? What ministries does it suggest to help young families? the expanding family? the shrinking family? newlyweds and senior citizens? What new dimension does it give to Christian education? What does it suggest for the winning and shepherding of new families? Small groups of parents meeting three or four times a year as study-discussion groups can make a major contribution to any parish. Neighborhood picnics of these families would help. *The priesthood of believers is a family affair!*

A well-known Bible commentator writes: "The New Testament is certain that the only training which really matters is given within the home, and there are no teachers so effective for good or evil as parents are . . . the child is the gift of God to the parent, and the child must be the gift of the parent to God."[3]

A public school superintendent says: "Parents have always overestimated the effect the schools have on the training and education of children. From birth through high school the child spends only 13 percent of his waking hours in school." He compares nurture to a three-legged stool: the home, the church, the school. If any of the three legs does not touch ground, education is not complete.[4]

"Unless churches become more concerned with and aware of the day-by-day religion that its members are living they will play an ineffectual and trivial role," writes Edith Hunter.[5]

In their book *The Church is Families* Edward and Harriet Dowdy write: "In the wisdom of God the home is still the major training unit in every individual's experience and parents are still the first teachers. More education has taken place before a child enters school than will be possible in any other five years of his life. . . . Like the watermark on stationery, every page of one's personal story is written against the background of his family."[6]

In its blueprint for Christian education the Presbyterian Church in the United States says: "The basic nurture of all church members of whatever age must necessarily be carried out in the household setting where the most elemental factors of life and death are met and the most intimate relationships established. . . . Unless this basic sort of nurture in the Christian faith is done here it is doubtful if it can be done at all effectively anywhere."[7]

In the light of Biblical injunctions and the testimony of outstanding educators, every church that believes in the priesthood of all believers needs to re-examine and re-align its educational philosophy and practice. Here is a man-size job for the church. *A family ministry is one of the first frontiers to be reclaimed by most churches.*

Unless the ministries outlined in this chapter are taken seriously and a realignment of priorities takes place, the "too exclusive concentration on the church as a worshiping, preaching, and sacramental institution will not get its much needed correction."[8]

CHURCHES WHICH ARE RECAPTURING MINISTRY BY GOD'S PEOPLE

Fortunately some new models of members in ministry with their pastor have given the activation of the laity a boost. We shall look at a few examples, beginning with the two churches most frequently cited.

The East Harlem Protestant Parish in New York City faced up to the facts of life in its community. It did not wish to remain a spiritual island for the faithful few.

It took seriously the ministry of its members as a practical operation. It wanted to be "the kirk in the world." That meant worship, instruction, and training to become "witnesses where you are." Members came together to be built up in the faith, but with the objective to be on mission in their own neighborhoods.

A door sticker about 6 inches square was designed with the words, "Welcome in the name of Christ" on the top, a symbol of clasped hands in the center, and the name of the parish on the bottom. Members of the parish posted it on the doors of their apartments. They wanted their neighbors to know that their home was open to them. As a result neighbors were welcomed and felt free to come in to talk about their needs, to study the Bible, to pray, to discuss neighborhood problems and ways of dealing with these constructively, in fact, to minister to each other in every kind of need.[9]

Another church which has put the priesthood of the laity into practice is the Church of the Savior in Washington, D. C. To fulfill their mission all members of the parish makes seven commitments.

"As an expression of my love for God, I will:

(1) Seek God's plan through a daily period of Bible reading and prayer.

(2) Worship weekly in the church and take Holy Communion.

(3) Participate weekly in group Bible study and the fellowship of prayer.

(4) Give regularly a definite, grateful share of my income for the spread of the kingdom through the church in the world.

"As an expression of love for my neighbor, I will:

(5) Pray daily for others with thanksgiving.

(6) Exercise faithfully my particular ministry in the fellowship of the church.

(7) Witness by word and deed in the world to the

love of God in Christ as I have come to know it.
So help me God!"[10]

A third church which has broken out of its institu-
tionalism is First Methodist Church, Germantown, Pa.
This church has been revitalized through small study
groups which seek fresh ways of expressing the new life
in Christ. It realizes that "most men in the modern
world will only discover the gracious God in and
through gracious neighbors, creating a veritable neighborhood of grace in the world," the kind that can be
found only in Christ."[11]

Coral Ridge Presbyterian Church, Fort Lauderdale,
Fla., is another example of putting the laity to work,
especially in evangelism. In 9 years this congregation
has become the fastest growing congregation of its
church body. It has a peak attendance of 2,850 in four
morning services. It is led by D. James Kennedy and
four assistants. But the secret of its growth is not
preaching alone. It is due to the recapture of every-
member evangelism. The congregation is built on the
following principles:

(1) The church is a body under orders from Christ
    to share the Gospel with the whole world (Acts
    8:4).
(2) Laymen as well as ministers must be trained to
    evangelize. (Pastors are given to equip all
    members of the church for mission.)
(3) Ministers are not to be star performers (while
    others watch) but to be the coach of a well-
    trained and well-coordinated team.
(4) Evangelism is more caught than taught. It is
    learned by "on the job" training.
(5) It is more important to train a soul-winner than
    to win a soul. This is simply a matter of good
    arithmetic.

This pastor has two training periods a year, consist-
ing of class instruction, homework assignments, and on-

the-job training. Workers go out by threes. The third person being the recruit getting on-the-scene experience.[12]

God used a congregation in central Michigan to "light a fire" which has spread rapidly. Bethlehem Lutheran Church of Saginaw with two dedicated pastors began training clergy in an art now being applied by a number of seminaries. Over a two-year period 225 pastors were put through a field training program *under lay people* of the congregation. The "Kennedy technique" was used.

In one District over 3,000 lay people have gone through such training clinics. Its evangelism counselor says: "You can't lead someone else to Calvary without going there yourself." Evangelism is caught rather than taught![13]

Within 20 years Concordia Lutheran Church, San Antonio, Tex., has increased to 3,000 members. The secret of this church's growth is attributed by the pastor to the lay people, and by the lay people to their pastor. Pastor Guido Merkens enlists practically everyone in some form of ministry: teaching, witnessing, caring, singing, serving God by serving their neighbors, and doing all these things with contagious gladness in the Holy Spirit. One lay teacher calls each of his ninth graders every week. The church offers a great variety of services and enlists people for each one: the day care center, an elementary Christian school, the Vacation Bible school (911 enrolled in 1971), and an aggressive sports program. The personal involvement of a majority of the youth and adults puts the laity to work in hundreds of activities. "Saving faith is personal, but never private," says the pastor.[14]

To reach modern man we must be ready to hear what he is saying and make our purpose clear. We must show him that *faith is better than doubt, hope better than despair, love better than hate.*[15]

Henry P. Van Dusen sizes up man's dilemma in a single sentence: "So the man of the street stands today, rootless—a prodigious, overgrown, adolescent sapling, swayed by every wind of doctrine, without the rootage which might have furnished him with security and stability."[10]

"The Word became flesh and dwelt among us." The Gospel must still be wrapped up in a human being!

Chapter Nine

TRAINING LAITY FOR SERVICE

PASTORAL STEWARDSHIP OF MANPOWER

In the Swabian Alps of southern Germany is a little village named Upfingen, with its centuries-old church. When visiting it I was struck by a fresco on the wall near the door. The pastor of this Evangelical Church told me the story. After World War II an interior renovation and modernization program was undertaken. Under several coats of paint the workmen discovered a painting. It turned out to be a fresco of a "Christopher," evidently painted in pre-Reformation days. The congregation restored this painting. The church, Catholic and Evangelical, has one basic task—"making Christophers" (which means Christ-bearers) of its people. To what extent are our contemporary churches developing "carriers" of the Christ?

THE PASTOR'S STRATEGIC ROLE

The pastor's role and leadership are needed more than ever! The character of the congregation is very much determined by his image of the church. What type of ministry will he develop? Will he wear a shepherd's cloak only? Does he have only a "soul-keeping" image of his ministry? Will he also fulfill the role of a commissioner of people? On assuming a pastorate he will be wise if he reviews with the elders and the people the type of ministry that matches the New Testament pattern. A priority listing of tasks should arise out of a mutual review of work in the parish. What are the role expectations of the congregation? Are they the same as the role expectations of our Lord?

Pastors and Christian teachers are supplied to equip all of God's people for their ministry in whatever station they are in life and in all areas of life. Ephesians 4:11-12 gives us a basic directive. Today's English Version puts it well: "It was He [Christ] who 'gave gifts to men'; He appointed some to be apostles, others to be prophets, others to be evangelists, others to be pastors and teachers. He did this to *prepare all God's people* for the work of Christian service, to build up the body of Christ." In plain English, this means the pastor's role is not merely to "keep" people with Christ but to "develop" them for Christ's service in the church and in the world. Whether he knows it or not, a pastor is the "head" of a "seminary," a training school for workers. His most significant stewardship is not of money but of people. He is entrusted with a commission! (1 Corinthians 9:17).

Some years ago Professor Samuel Blizzard made a survey of the Protestant minister's image of his roles. He wanted to learn how pastors ranked their tasks first in regard to significance in their scale of values; then in regard to the amount of time they devoted to these ministerial tasks. Here is what he found:

Rank by "importance":	*Rank in "time given":*
(1) preacher	(1) administrator
(2) pastor	(2) pastor
(3) organizer	(3) preacher
(4) administrator	(4) organizer
(5) teacher	(5) teacher[1]

What does this tell us? We note that teaching occupies the last place in both lists. David Ernsberger comments: "The present hierarchy of ministerial preferences, with preaching at tne top and teaching at the bottom, would become simply untenable for everyone who came to espouse Protestantism's traditional conception of the ministry." He then refers to the intimate connection between preaching and teaching which is maintained in the New Testament.[2]

By our rather narrow concept of preaching as one-way communication, we would have to view almost all of Jesus' messages as being teaching rather than preaching. Most of the material which is recorded in the four Gospels consists of Jesus' teaching. His teaching was quite informal. It included parables, questions, dialog, and discussion. Jesus used a face-to-face method. It was personal and direct. It called for response. It was what we today call dialogical teaching.[3]

No single term of the five used by Samuel Blizzard describes the strategic role of the modern leader of a church. The term pastor-director is perhaps most suitable. The New Testament emphasizes the servant role. Above all he is to be an enabler, and equipper of God's people for their ministry wherever they are in life, in the church and in the world.

THE SELF-IMAGE OF CLERGY AND LAITY

Traditions lay a heavy hand on pastors and congregations. When a pastor comes to a new parish he has his best opportunity to talk about role expectations of the pastor and the people. Ephesians 4:11-12 is a good place to begin. That is also the strategic moment to set up a common major goal. Begin with the question: What is the chief objective of a Christian congregation according to the New Testament? As the new pastor and the congregational boards think through the needs of the congregation and the mission in the community, a new sense of direction can be given to a whole congregation.

Some internal problems will also come up for discussion. At times it is necessary to state the situation negatively.

We will not build an active laity
> if confirmation is a finishing school;
> if education is for children only;
> if mere church attendance is all that is required;
> if the impression is left that we have our faith "only to die by";
> if missions are for missionaries;
> if religion is something we delegate to our minister.

All of these half-truths are misrepresentations in the mind, and they work against a ministry of the laity.

The average church member goes to church in the mood of a spectator instead of a participant. Yet Christians are part of God's orchestra! They are not called merely to give financial support to the orchestra but to play an instrument! A bishop in Manchester, England, put it tersely: "There has been in the past the impression that laymen exist 'to believe, to pray, to obey, and to pay.'" An American churchman has said: "The church faces ecclesiastical suicide unless it makes some radical changes in its traditional attitude toward laymen."

"It is a surprising fact," says J. Bruce Weaver, "that the church has been so obtuse in recognizing that it is already on the inside of many otherwise impenetrable segments of society in the person of its members. We are just beginning to realize that the first business of the official church and its clergymen is that of equipping Christians, not to be (housebroken) church mice, but to be red-blooded men and women in every context of life . . . men and women who know they are priests of the living God and a part of His strategy for reconciling the world to Himself."[5]

The pastor holds the key! He can keep his people merely as members on a church roll, or he can make them member-ministers.

Dr. Kenneth Cober says: "There is no such thing as being a member of the church without also being a 'minister' and a 'missionary'. . . . Essentially, the layman and the clergyman do not belong to different categories. But both have received and responded to the call of Christ and have given Him a basic commitment of their lives. The major differences lie in the fact that the clergyman gives his life in service to the church as his occupational vocation, spends more time preparing for his ministry, and performs certain functions that the church requires of its pastoral ministers. Otherwise the layman has no less responsibility for fulfilling his ministry than has the pastor."[6]

THE PASTOR AS TEACHER AND ENABLER

Where the pastor regards his people as member-ministers, he will no longer be satisfied with mere audiences but is compelled to alter his ministerial priorities to give every member a better understanding of his roles in home, church, and job as a member-minister. This is not an easy task. Some very comfortable old images must be destroyed and new self-images built up. With church traditions so firmly entrenched, the initiative and leadership must come from the pastor. He can begin with his board of elders, board of education, and the officers and leaders of all classes and organizations, from the nursery department to the senior citizens class. Change will not come quickly or easily. But the pastor will be amply repaid as he experiences a new sense of unity, fellowship, and joy in the people of his parish.

We have a Canadian layman's evaluation of church and ministry in the words of William Hinson: "The church as an institution will live, but it can no longer live as a spiritual outpatient clinic where men go on Sunday morning to get a holy dose of religious sedative. It must be a drill hall and a barracks, sending its soldiers out into the world as Christian businessmen, Christian doctors, lawyers, advertising men, journalists, salesmen. It's not the minister's task to bear the burden alone of Christian witness for his people. He's the quarterback calling the signals. It's their job to carry the ball. Unfortunately the minister does not always know what signals to call.'"

THE REBIRTH OF MINISTRY

We have too long depended on the sermon alone to do what it cannot fully do. It is indeed a central and vital part of our worship, because it is our shepherd communicating God's Word to us and making it relevant to our needs, times, people, circumstances. The purpose of the sermon is to instruct and inspire. But it is *not* a "drill hall." It is *not* "setting up exercises." It is *not* a "field trip" into the community.

No one has driven this point home more effectively than James Smart in his book *The Rebirth of Ministry*. He distinguishes sharply between members of an audience or organization and "disciples of Christ." "Jesus was not interested merely in having a succession of audiences to which either He or someone on his behalf might proclaim the Gospel. He was interested primarily in having disciples in whom and through whom his ministry would be multiplied many times over. . . . The preaching of the Gospel merely brings men to the threshold of discipleship. If they are to cross the threshold and become, in the true sense, disciples, that is learners or students, they must have a teacher. The two terms are correlative, disciple and teacher, and where there is no teacher but only a preacher, one need not expect to find disciples."[8] Again, he writes: "A preaching and pastoral and priestly ministry may build large congregations and impressive organizations, but only when there is added to them an effective teaching ministry does the church begin to become a fellowship of disciples."[9]

This author does not wish to downgrade preaching or disregard the importance of truly Biblical and evangelical teaching of the fundamental truths of the Gospel and an adequate understanding of the sacraments. He is saying that real teaching-learning is best achieved in the small study-discussion group, not in a worship assembly, not very effectively in any lecture-type presentation. With that most Christian educators will agree. Personal study is *vital*. Participation and discussion are *necessary*. But the goal is greater than knowledge and belief alone. The aim is *belief that leads to action*—a whole life directed to mission and ministry to people—those very close to us, members of our own family, and people in our congregation, in our community, and in the whole world.

TRAINING PROGRAM VITAL

This makes the *training program* as vital as the *preaching program*. Both need to be tied closely to the church's work program. Training should be for specific work programs: meeting new neighbors, reclaiming inactive members, winning whole families, reaching modern youth, and the like. Actual practice is a necessity. Our priesthood requires a practical apprenticeship under successful kingdom workers.

Workers should know not only what the Christian faith is but also *why it is so vital for all aspects of life in our times*. They need to be clear on the chief points of

Christian doctrine and be able to witness to the assurance, joys, and power of the Gospel in their own lives. Every church member needs experience in meeting people where they are and at their level of need.

The Christian worker needs empathy, a feeling of identification with the person he meets, an outgoing concern for people. These skills can be learned only by direct participation in missionary and service tasks. Witnessing is learned by doing. Evangelism calls for on-the-job training. New members are apprenticed to experienced workers. *It starts with giving specific neighborhood mission call assignments.*

EXAMPLES OF FUNCTIONAL TRAINING

A Kansas City church starting its work in a rented storeroom has grown through the years because it learned early to put its people to work. A Bible class grew because its members were divided into ten small teams of five to ten persons. Each team had a captain making weekly personal or telephone contacts with the teammates and the unreached. In this way over 100 persons were contacted each week. This church developed a sense of mission with its inductive studies in the Bible, always closely related to its work in the community. The weekly friendly call and the larger fellowship suppers developed a unity and spirit that helped to give the whole parish a witnessing character. Its contact with a Bible woman in India and a blind boy in China gave it a mission consciousness as did its Bible portion distribution program and Bible reading survey in the community. This mission church selected a group named "The Seventy" to make evangelism calls.

A small altar guild and ladies aid explored ways of enlisting the whole womanpower of the parish. It learned about the neighborhood circle plan. Ten geographical areas were selected. Two leaders were chosen for each circle. These 20 leaders worked out the program. The study and service ideas grew out of such questions as: What is a woman? What is a Christian woman? What are her basic needs? How can we help all of our women grow up into Christ and serve Him where they are? After considering many suggestions the women decided to have five missionary topics and five family related topics each year. These were worked out with the women, not for the women. Each circle chose its own name and service projects. There was no more joining a women's organization. All women of the parish were members because they belonged to the parish. The women's participation rose from 25 percent to 95 percent. The structure and basic philosophy were sound!

A St. Louis pastor asked a question: "Our church has received thirty-nine adults in the past year by instruction in Christian doctrine. What can we do for them now?" This was a basic question, because many churches "just receive them." How can they be assimilated? be a part of the fellowship? be equipped for their Christian mission? Knowing doctrine was not enough for that pastor! Out of this situation grew what came to be known as *The Discipleship Series,* five leadership training texts with five group leaders' manuals. Note the way the titles were phrased: (1) "Learning to *Use* Your Bible"; (2) "Christians *Worship*"; (3) "The Christian's *Mission*"; (4) "Christian *Family* Living"; (5) "The Church *Since Pentecost.*"

It was a layman on the board of an evening leadership training school, with fall and spring semesters, who suggested planning something special for Christian men to equip them better for leadership and service roles. This led to the holding of "Churchmen's Retreats" over Friday to Sunday weekends. The response was excellent. The program called for Bible study on the main theme, panel discussions, fellowship, and meditation periods. The themes were always related to God's people at work in the world. Here are a few of them:

"The Priesthood of All Believers,"
"Effective Ministry of Pastor and People,"
"The Christian and His Community,"
"Deepening the Spiritual Life,"
"Christian Man in Today's World,"
"Christ Meets the World in You,"
"The Pulpit in Your Life,"
"Let the Church Be the Church."

The question arose: How can we carry what we have learned and experienced back to our churches? In answer, a new format was chosen. Twelve churches were served at each retreat. Planning began with the selection of 12 pastors and joint planning with them. Each brought 10 laymen to the retreat. At the retreat the assignments were given to these congregational groups. New insights were gained. More effective plans of operation were designed. Most of the churches carried through a similar process with a larger number of parishioners.

LEARNING FROM THE MISSION FIELD

In New Guinea a central mission school was set up to serve 19 communities. Literacy courses, Bible stories, and basic Christian doctrine were taught. Due to the shortage of teachers only one of every eight children from each community could be accommodated. However, the teacher had a wise plan. He directed the children to retell what they had learned to the other children when they returned to their homes on weekends, using Bible story pictures. In this way a second and larger group of children was reached each week. This strategy resulted in mass baptisms. This built-in pattern of multiplying the workers was the secret of the phenomenal growth in New Guinea. What an object lesson for American churches![10]

David A. Womack asserts: "The only hope for the

total evangelization if the world is to teach the Christian believers of each nation to evangelize their own people and to incite in each country the conditions in which spontaneous lay movements of church expansion may occur. In short, the Church must abandon its stained-glass sanctuaries and take the gospel out into the streets."[11]

EVANGELISM CLINICS FOR SEMINARIANS

Under the leadership of a district director of evangelism some significant training has been given to theological students. The clinic is held in connection with an evangelism program in one or more parishes. By the use of films, Bible study, discussion of procedures, and reports of lay workers in the congregation the students get basic orientation. But the climax comes as seminarians go out with experienced laymen or women and learn firsthand how to present Christ's invitation to unchurched adults and their families.

One seminarian in reporting on the experience said: "This opened my eyes and gave me direction in evangelism; it gave me a real desire to share the Gospel; it provided an opportunity for true Christian fellowship with a lay partner; it exposed me to 48 hours of thinking, talking, and living the Gospel; it gave me new motivation for prayer, and greatly strengthened my own faith."

Other students gave similar evaluations: "parts of the clinic spent with laymen were the greatest"; "evangelism is a one-to-one expression of faith which can be learned only by actual experience"; "the expertise helped me to see how much a living relationship to Christ can mean to people"; "the only way to learn the program is to do it"; "the material was helpful (not just pious), purposeful, and offered some options." If the local parish is to teach its people evangelism then it must set up similar learning projects. We learn by *doing!*[12]

THE SELF-UNDERSTANDING OF THE LAITY

One denominational commission on mission and ministry found many hurdles as it approached local churches. It put its finger on a crucial point when it reported:

> No amount of change in the structure of the church, no multiplication of boards and commissions will have any lasting and radical effect on the church's mission if the individual Christian does not come to a proper understanding of his calling in the body of Christ. As long as the laity considers itself to be a passive element in the church to be served by the professional clergy the institutional self interest of the church is bound to be dominant over the essential character of the church as the mission of God to the world.[13]

After studying a set of comprehensive "Mission Affirmations" one adult Bible class reported that the average church does not with its regular program equip its members for mission and ministry but rather diverts its members into secondary goals and tasks. It questioned whether the church staff was equipped to do such training on a regular and consistent basis. Better clergy-laity relations are needed if people and pastor are to work as a team. The whole parish would need to rethink its basic goal and put outreach and service tasks above mere survival and church maintenance tasks. Parish members (not just the men or the faithful women or the pastor alone) would need to help determine the goal of the parish and help give the congregation a new sense of direction. The training experiences would be like those reported by the seminarians. Altogether too much of the work load has been put on the shoulders of pastors. Achievement of Christ's commission given to all Christians can be a possibility *only as pastor and people form a mission team.*

CHURCHES ARE LAUNCHING PADS

Christ at His ascension gave the church a basic strategy for the fulfillment of its mission. He described it as a movement of the church in ever widening circles. It is diagrammed for us in Acts 1:8. He said, "The Holy Spirit will empower you for witness from Jerusalem to Judea, to Samaria, to the ends of the earth!"

At Cape Kennedy the launching apparatus has projected the astronauts into space sending them to the moon on their now famous missions. Each local church is also such a launching site called by God to put its members into orbit for Christ right where they are in hundreds of vocations and locations.

Pontifex is a Latin term which means "bridge-builder." All of God's people are to be building bridges to people. They in fact are the "bridges" over which Christ Himself comes to men!

*Chapter
Ten*
ENLISTING GOD'S PEOPLE

THE EFFECTIVE USE OF VOLUNTEERS

Christian men and women are already on the front lines in their vocations, social relationships, and community enterprises. In this chapter we will deal with their roles as members of a Christian parish. The congregation, as we have noted, should not only be a *gathering* agency but also a *deploying* agency.

Thousands of church members are at work inside their congregations—as department leaders and teachers in Sunday school and vacation Bible school; as leaders of youth and adult classes and groups of men, of women, of couples. Your roster of church officers and administrative boards shows many other workers who assume responsibility for church buildings, salaried personnel, missions at home and abroad.

One important category is missing from this list: the congregation's field workers, the people who make community canvasses, visit new residents, seek out new families, or go on every-member visitations. A common term used for community chest and neighborhood canvass workers is "volunteers."

VOLUNTEERISM STARTED IN THE CHURCH

At a meeting of district directors of Christian education, a staff assistant of the Voluntary Section Center of the Health and Welfare Council of St. Louis said:

> The church cannot possibly exist without the help of its volunteers. The church above all agencies has the unique mission of involving its membership. As the church expands its role, more and more training and expertise are needed. Often the paid staff is afraid and/or unwilling to delegate some of its tasks to the so-called nonprofessional. If leaders are to be effective they must recognize the contribution the nonprofessional layman has to give. Volunteers not only enhance what is being done, they enable all leaders in the church to do a better job. Many a good church member has been left dormant because he was not asked to use his talents and capabilities. As a result his interests were channeled elsewhere.
>
> Actually the church was the nucleus for community services. The church volunteers established the hos-

pitals. The first kindergartens were held in churches. Social work started in the church. As these services became professionalized they became separate agencies. Many persons give their best working talents to a hospital, a community program, the scouting program, and a host of civic, business, and professional organizations.[1]

When we look outside the church we are amazed at the thousands of men and women from all vocations who are giving volunteer services to worthwhile causes. The annual community fund drives are such an example. People feel honored to serve in such projects. It has become a notable trait of American citizenship.

There are a number of sociological reasons for this wide response. Americans today have more leisure than their founding fathers. The automobile has given us our mobility. Mechanization in factory, office, and home has freed us for more volunteer services. Higher education has distributed expertise in many fields to millions of people. The number of retired persons has grown voluminously. They have the time and the talents to contribute significantly to church and civic enterprises. People want to be busy at challenging tasks. Thousands of adults volunteer their help in the annual Red Cross drive. It gives them community status and neighborhood recognition.

There are deeper reasons too. Someone put it aptly. Giving our time and talents for a worthwhile cause is "the rent we pay for occupying our station in life." People don't want to be receivers only, or only auditors and onlookers. They want to be where the action is!

The church must understand that it is not an agency to be served but a work force to be deployed. Unfortunately the work force of the church often is relatively small and static. Literally millions of its members will never have an opportunity to do the basic work of the church, *chiefly because they have not been asked, motivated, directed, and used.*

"Church as usual" where nothing but you and your pocketbook are expected has failed to give Christ the workers He needs. Nor does it square with the dynamics of the Gospel. Christianity is a "happening," not just a theory in the limbo of the mind.

Volunteerism began in the church. It should be a natural consequence of belonging to the people of God. In fact, the church can't exist without the help of volunteer workers. In a sense volunteers are more valuable than paid staff, since *no staff is big enough to do the job that needs to be done.* There is a personal touch in the work of laymen, or to put it in another way, there is no "professionalism," no feeling such as, "That's what we expect from a pastor." Properly motivated and evangelically trained the layman has a certain authenticity about his work for Christ; he is not being paid for it. Without a core of lay workers how else could a parish get into its own neighborhood?[2]

THE MIMEOGRAPH CAN'T DO IT

In most churches the mimeograph is "overoperative" because the lay force is "underoperative." A volunteer parish worker in a Kansas City church gave at least one day of service every week making calls in the community. This worker was the main "contributor of people" to an adult Christian instruction program and to Sunday school and Vacation Bible school enrollments.

Neither preaching, nor formal teaching, nor an occasional evangelism drive can take the place of the regular lay activity, week by week, that reaches into the homes of the people of the community. Even the pastor needs such activity to strengthen his morale and overcome moments when he feels his aloneness. A parish gets a new sense of unity when people and pastor in reality are a working team. But this means that *the wider use of the laity* for the basic functions of the church *must be fully accepted as a congregational polity!*

"The church unconsciously is aiding secularization when she encourages private piety apart from public responsibility," says David Schuller, and then adds: "The question of social responsibility is not a pleasant extra for the church in an affluent age; it is the heart of the question of how the church can give witness to people as they live, work and play in our society."[3]

WHAT SERVICES ARE NEEDED

Just a minimal listing of leadership needs in a parish is almost frightening. Leaders are needed for:

> The Church schools: Sunday, weekday, vacation schools.
>
> Youth and adults: program planning, officers and leaders.
>
> Study and action: Bible class departments and group leaders.
>
> Special projects: congregational visitation, welcome new residents moving into community, evangelism (like the year-long Key 73 program); visitation of shut-ins and the sick; social welfare projects in the larger community.
>
> Service and Christian growth groups—for parents, young adults, married couples, men's groups, women's groups, mission study and work groups, home and foreign mission projects.
>
> Ministry to families: the founding, expanding, empty-nest families.
>
> Music-Worship program: organists, accompanists, choir members and leaders.

Every parish will need to rethink its major goals and set up its new projects year by year and assess what kind of volunteers will be needed for each project.

WHAT MAKES A GOOD VOLUNTEER?

Each class or age group or study-work organization will need alert leadership; persons who are wide awake to the needs of people in the church and the community; people who have some background and experience or are capable of developing some dormant skills. Leaders are people who are alert, imaginative, deeply interested in a specific field of work and study; who move from study to action; people who inspire others and by their approaches to people convey confidence, give courage and incentive for action. Usually they will be people who are spiritually alive, mentally alert, and have a contagious interest in other people. They should inspire others with their ideas, faith, and way of life. They should be knowledgeable in the Bible, be able to express themselves clearly, have empathy—a warm feeling toward people—and a desire to do well everything they undertake.

Look for persons who can:
>   Meet people face to face,
>   learn to know them,
>   open up conversation,
>   feel at home with people,
>   share their own insights and hopes,
>   demonstrate love for people,
>   are ready to do something for them,
>   can establish good rapport.

The attitude of the worker and an outgoing personality are important. *Every church has such people!* Some are better prepared for teaching and for visitation work. All can learn and get new satisfaction from their assigned tasks—if they are well chosen and carefully groomed for their tasks.

Here is a challenging appeal to the institutional church: "Get rid of all the false frostings we have put on our religion. . . . Give our youth the truth. . . . Let them know that being a Christian is hard—it is exact-

ing, it is exciting, it is challenging, and it is a commitment that will, if we really live it, cost us our lives."[4]

FINDING AND ENLISTING THE WORKERS

Most churches do not know the resources they have
in their own members. We need a long enough visit with
each new member to learn the background, religious
education, general education, special training, and interests and experiences people bring with them into the
church fellowship. Does your church really know the
hidden talents and aspirations of all members? A talent
file with a card for each member will help if it is kept up
to date and used. A competent enlistment secretary,
close to the pastor and church office secretary, should
keep the file up to date. New members are honored if
they are visited to get some information and their background of experience, especially their individual interests.

The enlisting process should begin when people are
received as members. If they are not used they will follow the pattern of being audience only and will become
routine churchgoers but otherwise quiescent—*"because
no one has asked us."*

Your church probably has more college students and
graduates than in any previous decade of its history.
Have you located them? With some additional guidance
these people can become part of your volunteer force.
What is that teacher, that expert in business, that sales-
man, that nurse, that social worker, that community
worker doing in your parish? He or she must be sought!
The church task must be presented with challenge; or
else very soon the professional or civic service club will
have him or her. People need to be enlisted personally
by word of mouth, not by a form letter from the church
office or an announcement in the Sunday bulletin. Keep
in mind that money is no substitute for a person! God
wants the person to help build His kingdom. Actually

the institutional image most people have of the church can cheat your parish out of the help money can't buy!

THE ROLE OF THE ENLISTMENT SECRETARY

But who can do this vital piece of work in your church? Paul found, enlisted, trained, and used these: Timothy, Titus, Silas, Priscilla and Aquilla, Phoebe and Lydia. It's the personal touch that counts. The pastor can open the door for volunteer services or he can close the door. He should make the start. But in a church of several hundred youths and adults he will need to delegate this work to a well-chosen enlistment or assignment secretary. In a large congregation this secretary will need several helpers and work closely with all department leaders, committee chairmen, various groups who need leadership talent. The pastor, director of education, and enlistment secretary, meeting with leaders of all departments of the Sunday school and chairmen of all program developing groups, should discuss annually the kind and number of leaders needed for efficient operation. In large churches a full-time worker can take on this leadership selection and training task. Brief job descriptions are helpful in finding and directing qualified persons for specific tasks.

Workers who have accepted assignments will need proper briefing for the work they are to do. A good example is the briefing given for evangelism calls. Workers need to be called together, given clear direction, adequate background information, helpful materials, specific assignments, names, addresses, telephone numbers, and inspiration for their work.

Don't take your volunteer workers for granted. Train them well by assigning them to experienced workers. Where special leadership training is necessary—for a teaching assignment, for instance—direct them to time, place, and department. Give adequate help, for instance, in making effective telephone calls. And never forget to thank them for any service they have performed. An annual recognition dinner is a fitting tribute to them.

It is important that adequate records are kept of contacts made and a memo made for the pastor or department leader or chairman of a visitation program.

Tangible results are the best stimuli for more work: Families gained, children enrolled, new adults in the pastor's membership preparation class, youth, young families, new couples introduced to nearby fellow members of the parish. The greatest benefit will be a greater sense of purpose, fellowship, and unity in a growing church. A parish that uses its people in significant kingdom services gets a new sense of strength. Good rapport is vital. Reports of successful calls build up self-confidence.

HOW ONE CHURCH DOES IT

Practically every parish has in its membership a person who combines the gifts of a stenographer with the ability to meet people and work with a corps of volunteers. One pastor found such a person with an excellent background in church administration and put this experience to work in his parish.

He developed a special visiting program. Twice a month 7 to 10 women meet to take their assignment of calls to be made, usually about 50 each month. Each woman devotes several afternoons a week to the work of calling on new members, prospective members, the sick in hospitals, some shut-ins, and families with youth or with children in the Sunday school.

Each week five cassettes of the pastor's sermon are taken to persons who are no longer able to come to church. The cassette with tape recorder player are left by one person early in the week and after several days picked up by a second person to be taken to yet another shut-in. This system makes possible weekly contacts by *two* people with the same person.

A nearby neighborhood nursing home is visited every Monday. A cassette and player is left there also. The church visitor always takes a second person along—this provides in-service training for more workers. The visitors do errands for these shut-ins as part of their service. Other persons at the nursing home are invited to listen with them to the taped message.

A shepherding program is carried out by elders each with his own district. Each elder has two or three helpers. Visits are made to new members, inactive members, and prospective members. Each elder has about 50 persons to be visited three or four times a year. This program is headed by the president of the congregation.

The evangelism committee enlists canvassers who work in teams of two. Every year one or more geographical areas are surveyed in a house-to-house canvass. Adults and youth participate in this program of neighborhood witness.

A young single-adult group meets twice a month: one Sunday evening at the church, another in a home where a freer atmosphere encourages better participation. Parents work with the high school youth department during the Sunday school period and give help with weekday projects. A very active senior citizens group once a year entertains the youth groups partly because they relate well to teen-agers.

Practically every church has the lay personnel to carry out a similar program. The pastor of this parish says: "The personal touch does it!"⁵

THE RURAL CHURCH TOO!

Rural and small churches also need this dynamic kind of ministry. Farming has become big business. The small farm has given way to larger tracts of land (whole square miles) cultivated by modern power-driven machinery. There are fewer farm families, but they too need to be served for a more fruitful rural ministry. New strategies are now being developed in workshops for rural churches.

One such workshop for Manitoba and Saskatchewan churches attended by selected laymen and clergymen had the following objective: "To study ways and means of equipping and training the laity for a team ministry approach to multiple rural parishes." The agenda included discussions on:

> "The Mission of God's People in the New Testament,"
>
> "The Lay Ministry and Its Relation to the Pastoral Ministry,"
>
> "The Mission of God's People in the Multiple Parish,"
>
> "What Qualifications Are Needed for Lay Leadership?"
>
> "How Help Congregations Enlist, Develop, and Accept Lay Leadership?"
>
> "Materials and Methods for Training the Laity."

This workshop involved 10 carefully selected laymen, 10 pastors representing various geographical areas, 4 district mission directors, and 5 denominational resource leaders contributing insights from a theological seminary, a board of parish education, a junior college president, a director of a lay training institute, and a representative of the church body's board of missions.[6]

EVERY CHURCH NEEDS A TEAM MINISTRY

Most important is the development of a sense of co-responsibility by pastor and people. This means the enlistment of the whole man and the whole woman, with all of their training and experience. On the human side, this calls for enlistment, encouragement, instruction, and a genuine sense of confidence between pastor and people.

More important than setting up the annual monetary budget is an annual assessment of talent and an annual work program including new and old tasks. It should provide for a new recruitment of talent, a shifting of personnel as needed for a variety of tasks—all of this for the wisest deployment of lay workers. Without this we are in danger of heaping more work on already willing and competent church workers.

This would be a natural consequence as the congregation realistically (1) recognizes and uses persons as gifts of the Holy Spirit, (2) recognizes that it is an incorporation of the body of Christ in that place, (3) recognizes that gifts and talents grow as more people learn from experience as part of the working force in the parish.

"The church is true to its purpose as it both *gathers* and *disperses*. The church must stay together long enough to realize its purpose, then it must *pour itself out* to become the salt in the community and in the world.'"

LAY MINISTRY IS A NECESSITY

The development of a ministry of the laity is essential. It contributes to the personalization of faith. Only as people are enlisted personally in Christ's mission does a congregation experience "wholeness" and recover "brotherhood." A new birth includes life-commitment.

The attitude and expectancy of pastor and people are important. Pastors often hesitate to ask for more than church attendance. This is too low a goal. *Self-identification with Christ's mission, nothing less, is the goal. Growth to Christian maturity is the target. Incorporation into the body of Christ (the church) is true membership. To see only the organizational shape of the Church can mean death to a parish.*

"The day is long past when the clergy bore the whole

burden of the defense of the faith. A new age of the layman has dawned. *The strongest, most far reaching witness of the church must be that of laymen.* To be effective, this witness must be rooted in both experience and knowledge, in honest and thorough study of the Scriptures, of Christian history, of ethical principles, of general philosophy, of contemporary psychology, of other world religions."[8]

An ongoing enlistment of workers means moving from passivity and patronage to participation and activity; from the idea that we withdraw from the world into the church to the idea that in the church we are prepared for life in the world. It means moving from the concept that the congregation exists mainly for its own self-preservation to the concept of mutual mission and ministry. It means laymen trained for witness and service, not merely to be "church-maintenance men and women." It means openness to new and better ways of equipping God's people through practice and experience. It means moving from almost exclusively building-centered operations to neighborhood operations. Most of all it means helping more of God's people understand that the grace of God gives them freedom in Christ, freedom to live by the Gospel, *celebrating their priesthood in all areas of life.*

WHAT SHAPE OF A CHURCH DO WE WANT?

STRUCTURAL REORGANIZATION OF A PARISH

In recapturing the ministry of every Christian the churches of America have a major task. It is however a fundamental one. It is basic to any real renewal. It must be undertaken with both firmness and wisdom.

Some critics of the church ask for what is almost a revolution, discarding completely the old forms. We will do well to use moderation at this point. Past images and practices cannot be dealt with rudely or unsympathetically. We must begin where people are and move them to where they should go—on missions in their several worlds.

The church under any plan will retain an institutional image. The assembling of believers is a necessity. The mission concept Scripture gives us is not an option. It belongs to the essence of the church. Church and institution are not opposites. However, these assemblies of believers are not an end in themselves but a means to basic goals. The congregation is the "school" for the development of God's people. The church is the "toolhouse" for God's workers. It is an "armory" for God's soldiers. It is a "house of refuge" for the weary and oppressed. It is a "Lighthouse" for those on the stormy sea of life. It is a "power plant" that supplies the spiritual current which lights up our personal lives and through us spiritually "electrifies" church and society.

The individual Christian needs a church home and the shepherding of a pastor. The office of the pastor was never more vital than it is today. We would have something akin to confusion without such leadership. In this chapter we explore ways in which the local church can more effectively fulfill its mission through all of its members by operating with a structure that facilitates the priesthood of all believers.

WHAT DO WE WANT THE CHURCH TO BE?

We are rightly proud of our theological heritage yet much too closely attached to familiar old forms no longer adequate for the mission to be fulfilled. Just as our cities are being rebuilt with modern structures, so also the church from time to time needs to examine its structural shape. This begins with the basic theological images we have of the corporate church.

What do we want the church to be?

— a building? or living stones?
— a harbor? or a launching pad?
— a country club? or a service station?
— a settlement? or a group of pilgrims?
— a cave of refuge? or a new creation?

We also need to define "church success." Is it mainly a growing membership list and a growing budget adequately met? Is it new houses built or families strengthened? Is it a hard-working paid staff? Or is it many Christians ministering to each other and reaching the community with the Gospel in word and deed?

Even our definitions are involved. Does mission mean people at work here? or missions in far away places funded by our money? It should be both! Too often we visualize the church *only* in its organizational shape. This is not unimportant. But if we see nothing more, the church will exist to perpetuate its historic form. Fortunately these questions are being asked by whole denominations and by ecumenical Christendom. Hendrik Kraemer has some significant words for us:

> What can and must be said and resaid, with all gratitude for what in many places is already happening, is that a fearless scrutiny and revision of structure is one of the most urgent aspects of a renewal of the church. . . . Like all institutions, worldly or religious, the church is on its institutional side most resistant. In many respects churches are more recalcitrant to change than any other institution, because they have sacralized themselves."[1]

FUNCTION SHOULD DETERMINE FORMS

In many respects the local church is stronger than ever, says Gerald J. Jud, General Secretary, Division of Evangelism, United Church of Christ. It is beginning to recognize that the world has changed, that the present structure of the local church is no longer adequate, that it ministers to the private life, but has failed to establish a depth relationship with its members. It needs to establish more of the servant shape of its Lord and not attempt to "domesticate the God who goes before." It must practice brotherhood, not race and class discrimination. Worship dare not be detached from the agonies of the world of our day. "The forms of the life of the church should depend on function. They should be designed to facilitate locating and participating in the mission of God. This is not the situation now."

The laity are largely acting as assistants to the clergy in churchly performances. Instead the clergy's expertise should be used in helping the laity who are set in the midst of the world. The church is too concerned with its image as an institution. But things are changing. Across America churches are rediscovering their sense of mission right where they are. Congregations should become recruiting stations of people who must be the primary manifestation of the stream of history living out the Biblical message. In the local church new Christians come into being. Children, youth, and adults are incorporated into the "pilgrim people of God." The local church will remain the center for public worship. But its worship in so many instances is "far too cerebral." To this we can add "and too much building-oriented."

Actually the churches have many committed people in the world. The church needs to stand alongside of persons and organizations with a new sense of confidence in the laity and more realistic, life-related, dialogical teaching and preaching. We all must help the church respond creatively to the real world of our day with the Christian Gospel and with the Christian way of life.[2]

CHURCH AND MINISTRY IN TRANSITION

In the last three decades the churches in the world have been reexamining their theological, historical, and missionary premises. They have done this largely in the light of the church's mission and ministry in a world passing through cataclysmic changes comparable to those of the Renaissance and the 15th century Reformation. The focus today is on the relation of the Gospel to the church's task at the close of the 20th century. A secretary of South Asia missions asks: "Have we perhaps closed our eyes to the fact that in our day the congregational shape of the parish is stiff, formal, and muscle-bound? That it tends more to insulate *from* the world than to equip the saints *for* ministry *in* the world?" Then he suggests that the answers we are led to by the Book of Acts might be in terms of a cell ministry, or a house church, or a group of five to eight congregations with an assortment of gifts (personal) more suitable for equipping all of God's people for their ministry where they are in today's society![3]

It is the ministry of the laity which is of paramount importance in the contemporary situation. *The church is facing a losing battle unless it equips its laity for mission where they are in life.* Frequently however the church directs and trains them for secular functions in the church structure, the housekeeping chores, or as assistants to the clergy.[4]

Reformation is never easy. The people who followed the Reformers found themselves with traditions many centuries old. They were closely linked to a hierarchical structure. The congregational polity which the Reformers espoused could not be completely achieved. For centuries parish priests had been placed by their bishops. Moreover the whole system of the church was inextricably interwoven with secular governments. Separation of church and state is an American achievement. In certain countries complete congregational autonomy waited until the middle of the 20th century.[5]

REEXAMINE YOUR GOALS

Renewal begins with a penetrating quest for the cardinal purpose of the church drawn from the life of the first-century Christian as recorded in the Acts of the Apostles. We need to make an in-depth inquiry into such questions as: Does our program of ministry to our congregation maintain a proper balance between nurturing the lives of our members and training them for mission and ministry? Does the teaching-learning experience, as carried on at all age levels, provide an adequate enounter with the Bible, the church, God, the world, one's own self, and others? Have we made the church entrance form a sort of graduation instead of a commencement? Do pastor and parishioners continually discover specific needs in the community for particular witness and helpful services? Have we put too much confidence in preaching and overrated its capacity to develop a corps of workers who will help carry out the full complement of services and functions illustrated for us in the ministry of our Lord and His apostles?[6]

The pastor is the key man. By his personal and aggressive ministry he can start writing a new chapter of the congregation's history. *He must be honest enough to recognize what preaching alone can do and cannot do; and add the structures, forms, experiences, and exercises that can develop his people into living, working, witnesses to the Gospel.*

The pivotal role of the pastor is underscored by J. Donald Butler, who says: "On him rests the burden to bring authenticity into the organization and life of the congregation. . . . He is the servant of the historic church. He is, as it were, at the center of the life of the congregation in a way in which no other person is, and there is a sense in which he can speak for the body of the church in a way that no other person can.'"

WHAT CHURCH-IMAGE DO YOUR MEMBERS HAVE?

The best way to find out is to make an actual survey with a carefully selected sample of your people. Decide: who should be included? how many adult men? adult women? young adult couples? college and high school youth? older members of the parish? newer adult accessions to the parish? In addition select a number of representative families who will be asked to make a joint reply. Your sample should include three categories of church members: regular and active members, persons who only come to church services, and persons who seldom come to church. Select your questions carefully— not too many, but everyone of them significant. One should relate to family religious practices (Bible use, family and private devotions, prayer practices). One or more questions should cover personal witnessing, contacts with neighbors and friends, fellow workers, relatives. The analysis should be made by the pastor and a select committee and the evaluation further discussed by a representative group of parishioners including your church council. Such a parish survey should suggest some new priorities. It will help you discuss weaknesses and strengths. It may reveal basic omissions in your present program. What processes, services, teaching and training methods need to be strengthened? Which functions and operations should be modified or dropped? (For more comprehensive studies see the magazine *The Christian Ministry,* January 1973, which focuses the entire issue on "measuring ministries and resources for evaluation."[8]

TOWARD A MORE FUNCTIONAL STRUCTURE

To simplify the work of an over-organized church, to help the under-organized parish, and to provide a better balance (priorities diagram "A" is submitted on pages 128 and 129. It attempts to reflect the main assignments of the New Testament for the last decades of the 20th century.

Most church constitutions are oriented to the business operations and survival goals of a parish. They also reflect a heavy emphasis on the doctrinal-theological stance of the denomination, but frequently they are weak in stating the functional goals of a church and the media for their achievement. Many parishes go on for years without comparing their constitution with the mission given in the New Testament. They go on with a business-as-usual attitude and largely on the basis of traditions long operative in the congregation. In many churches the business meetings are almost exclusively confined to the operation of the physical church plant, the funds needed, and the adoption of the annual budget. Survival aims are more prominent than mission and ministry aims. Usually the educational and leadership training programs are too restricted in scope and again more survival-centered than mission-centered, that is, concerned chiefly with meeting budgets, keeping up buildings, holding members.

The diagram is supplied to produce helpful discussion. It should help you rethink the priorities in your congregation. Do they need to be reexamined? Is your Christian education and leadership training program sound? ongoing? functional and fruitful? or practically nonexistent? At least once each decade every local church should take a fresh look at itself and include in its evaluation team the young adults added to the parish in the last 10 years. The congregation needs to be courageous enough to throw out what is weak and put in what is missing. And this should be done in the light of the apostolic mission given to us in the New Testament. Are such items as family ministry, mutual care, neighborhood circles, ongoing evangelism and Christian social welfare receiving adequate attention throughout each year?

Good administration is significant. Does your business agenda make "housekeeping" the main business of most meetings? Is as much time and thought devoted to the enlistment department, to talent discovery and development in leadership training? How many new people are groomed for an expansion of your ministry to your own people and to the people of your community?

Once a year, take time at all officers' and elders' meetings (of all groups from board of elders to Sunday school staff, youth council, Scouting leaders, women's groups, etc.) to study and discuss the diagram. What does it say to your parish? Does it suggest a new set of priorities? How broad is your program of nurture? How extensive is your leadership training program? Is it ongoing? Are learn-by-doing methods employed? What percent of your congregation is being trained for the services listed in column four of the diagram? Do you have adequate personnel (such as an enlistment secretary) to activate many more of your members? Administration is placed in column five because the first four columns deal with the basic mission and ministry tasks. It is disturbing indeed to go to a congregational assem-

1. WORSHIP	2. NURTURE	3. TRAINING
Congregational Sacraments.	Education Agencies	Enlistment for Services
Groups	Classes	Learning Leadership:
Classes	Premembership Bible	Teaching
Schools	Doctrine	Group Work
		Home Visitation
		Family Services
Personal Family	Way-of-Life Mission	
		Personal Evangelism
Confirmations	Men	Retreats
Installations	Women	Workshops
Weddings	Couples/Parents	Library
Funerals	Youth	
	Children	Assignments
	Pre-School	
Pastor	Pastor/ Dir. Chr. Ed.	Pastor/ Dir. Chr. Ed.
Ushers	Heads of All Teaching Agencies	Librarian
Choirs	Teachers, Leaders	
Organist	All Ages	Enlistment secretary
Altar Guild	Children, Youth, Adults	
Board of DEACONS	Board of CHRISTIAN NURTURE and LEADERSHIP TRAINING	
ALL Communicant Members form the CONGRE		

4. MINISTRY	5. ADMINISTRATION	6. COORDINATION
Pastoral care/ counseling	Congregational ASSEMBLY	◀ Leaders of Areas 1-5 meet quarterly
Visitations— Sick, Needy, Inactive, Unchurched	Reports of all Departments	—to review —to strengthen —to coordinate —to plan
Family Services	Church Growth Church Finance	
Neighborhood Groups, Circles	Church Office Plant Maintenance	Call together the leaders of ALL Departments,
Fellowship Gatherings	Equipment Library	Agencies, Groups —to develop
Community Surveys	Annual Parish Program	Annual Parish GOALS and Year's
Ongoing Evangelism	Denominational—	Parish Program
Social Welfare	World Mission	—Evaluation
Pastor/Church Council	Officers of Parish	◀ These leaders form the "WORK-ING STAFF"
Enlistment Sec.	Trustees, Elders	meet biannually To Evaluate Revise
Leaders of all Christian Services and Action Groups	Heads of ALL Boards and Working Groups	Project New Projects
Board of FIELD SERVICES	Board of CHURCH Management and Finance	◀ These BOARDS form the CHURCH COUNCIL

GATIONAL ASSEMBLY (2 or 3 meetings a year)

bly and find 90 percent of the time used for housekeeping subjects (column 5) and 10 percent for mission and ministry tasks (columns 1-4).

SOME QUESTIONS TO ASK

No two congregations will have the same organizational structure. Often the constitution and bylaws are a half century old. Has anyone evaluated them for guiding the church in our times? Are your priorities the right ones? Do they embrace the mission our Lord gives to the church? Are they geared to the close of the 20th century?

What is the ratio of full-time workers to members volunteering their services? Is the staff substituting for lay workers, or is it enlisting, training, directing, and evaluating an increasing number of the parish members for the congregation's work program?

How broad is your program of field services? How large is your voluntary field force? Should it be expanded? Is it wisely directed? Are people happier because they serve? Are fellowship and love for service growing? Are pastor and people working together as a team?

What percent of your youth and adult membership are involved in the annual meeting of your whole congregation? Is the womanpower as well as the manpower adequately enlisted and used? Are the congregation and its leaders open to suggestions? Are ample opportunities for sharing constructive ideas offered? In your business agendas, do survival and maintenance goals outnumber training and service goals?

Is the whole parish involved in program development by means of a coordinating council that meets once or twice a year? Is the sense of mission waning or growing in your congregation?

A DIFFERENT APPROACH

There are other equally valid approaches to congregational structure. One that deserves special attention is found in Robert C. Worley's book *Change in the Church: A Source of Hope.* It is based on the dynamics of organizations as living systems. It describes how interrelated groups contribute to a common goal. No group, committee, or service is autonomous, independent, isolated, and without effect for other boards, agencies, and operations of the parish. When any group in the church loses concern for any other group, the whole congregation becomes sick and real unity is threatened.

Dr. Worley's diagram (see page 132) consists of three "systems": an "input system" which recognizes historical and existential influences already extant and the pooled resources of the people, such as educational materials, money, and other values. Under the term "transforming system" he lists worship services, educational processes, various study and work groups, mission projects, and leadership development programs. He uses the term "output system" for task forces, mission involvements, and adults, youth, and children better equipped for mission and ministry. Both clergy and laity are God's change agents!

The manner in which a congregation thinks of itself is more vital than we think. Structure can create or destroy persons and the realization of plans. It can encourage, stimulate, and enlist participation. It can awaken new creativity and enthusiasm, or it can kill interest. Good structure is important. The quality of the people who administer the program and their spirit of cooperation and enthusiasm are even more important!

DIAGRAM B

From *Change In the Church; a Source of Hope,* by Robert C. Worley. Copyright © MCMLXXI, The Westminster Press. Used by permission.

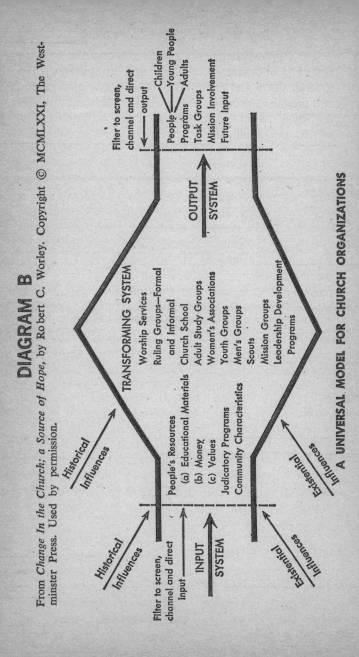

A UNIVERSAL MODEL FOR CHURCH ORGANIZATIONS

Historical Influences

Filter to screen, channel and direct input

INPUT SYSTEM

Existential Influences

People's Resources
(a) Educational Materials
(b) Money
(c) Values
Judiciary Programs
Community Characteristics

TRANSFORMING SYSTEM

Worship Services
Ruling Groups—Formal and Informal
Church School
Adult Study Groups
Women's Associations
Youth Groups
Men's Groups
Scouts
Mission Groups
Leadership Development Programs

Historical Influences

OUTPUT SYSTEM

Existential Influences

Filter to screen, channel and direct output

People
Children
Young People
Adults
Programs
Task Groups
Mission Involvement
Future Input

The output systems in some church organizations are the most unorganized, chaotic, and troublesome. The individualism and separatism of persons, committees, and organized groups can just about wreck a parish. On the other hand, unity of purpose, commitment to Christ, and intelligent, cooperative churchmanship can make a parish a mighty force in the whole community. Worley asks: "Is the health, character or climate of the church organization a visible expression of the Christian faith?" Are mistrust, alienation, hostility undermining the congregation? Dr. Worley admits that much teaching and preaching are not significant enough to produce the God-intended results. *Church services can be well attended and the annual budget oversubscribed, but without significant personal, spiritual growth, concern for fellow members, and the fulfillment of the church's world mission.* Both clergy and laity need to work in unison toward common goals if the church's mission is to be fulfilled.[9]

Good plans can go unused. They can gather dust on the drawing board. An announcement in the Sunday bulletin will not implement them. The conviction of ministers that what is preached on Sunday has a direct influence on what listeners do on Monday is a delusion, says Peter Berger. The sermon has many values, but it does not as a rule enlist workers or train them for action. Something more is needed; the direct person-to-person work of an enlistment secretary. *The church of Jesus Christ has a tremendous talent pool of largely unenlisted and unused people.*

HOW ONE CHURCH DID IT

Church renewal is needed by every congregation. *Unity* and *purpose* become real again only as both are "reborn" in the minds of laity and clergy. Old forms have a way of fading away. They can lose relevance as a church moves into another era. *We live in such a new era!*

But how to achieve renewal for laity and clergy? One way is to start with some basic mission affirmations and develop a new congregational constitution. This is the approach one church used. It set out to write a working, functional constitution and involve the whole congregation at some point of the process. Sample new constitutions of other parishes were examined. Much was learned from them. After only three meetings of the committee, the pastor accepted a call to another parish. The committee kept at its task over a 9-month period and for 6 months met weekly during the Sunday school hour. During this time the members of the congregation were invited to come and give their suggestions to the committee. This constitution was written in down-to-earth, functional terms. Much attention was given to the basic goal. Five basic purposes were chosen as constituting the goal:

(1) Worship—to exhibit being the body of Christ, and building each other up for witness to Christ's Lordship in every area of life.

(2) Nurture—to equip all members through teaching-learning for their ministry as members of the body of Christ.

(3) Fellowship—to commune with our Lord in the Lord's Supper and with each other for our mutual growth in Christ.

(4) Evangelism—to call upon each baptized member to be a daily witness to Christ and to participate in the worldwide mission.

(5) Service—to practice our Christian calling under the lordship of Christ in our daily work, home life, church work, community services in demonstration of the Gospel at work in our lives.

All of these statements are abbreviations of more complete paragraphs in the finished constitution.

But good aims are never enough. The real test comes in converting them into action in the life of the congregation and its individual members. This was done by setting up a director (a layman or woman) and a committee for each of the five areas defined above and dividing the work into several areas to implement a goal more adequately. In the area of *nurture* there are three directors and their committees: a director of *discipleship,* concerned mainly with spiritual well-being, mutual fellowship and leadership training; a director of *education,* concerned with the well-rounded growth in "knowing and living" of all children, youth, and adults; and a director of *youth,* concerned with ministry by youth and to youth, talent development and use, and the involvement of the parents. In the area of *service* there are two directors and committees, one in the area of *social ministry,* welfare, community affairs, citizenship; another in *stewardship*—individual enlistment in the full stewardship of all of life for Christ and His cause.

It is significant that the stewardship committee is instructed to give serious thought each year to (1) What is God's purpose for this congregation in this community? (2) What is God's purpose for each member in his circumstances?

Of course, adopting a paper document does not mean renewal. The planning committee recognized that renewal could come only as all members of the parish *identified themselves with the common goal.* Under the leadership of the new pastor, the goals were identified and clarified. A second significant step was taken: a visitation of all members. The visitation theme was "Call and Listen." The purpose was to develop a better acquaintance between members, to learn the needs and concerns of individuals, and to show real concern for the persons visited. This type of call awakened a new interest in the mission of this old congregation to its own members and to its work in the community.

The congregation realized that frequent every-member visitations needed to be a part of the main strategy of the congregation. The visiting teams, with assignments for responsibility for persons living in a given geographical area of the congregation, became a permanent part of a "shepherding program." Mutual ministry was being experienced.

One worker summarized the whole operation of writing a new constitution (sharing it with the members) and the family visitations as "a story of people who have learned to live their faith in mutual concern for each other." The shepherding program involves at least three calls a year: one to establish good rapport and a new concern for each other, one to enlist members in some phase of kingdom service in church and community, and another to enlist adequate support for the congregation's work program at home and abroad. The real goal was not money subscriptions but fellow Christians involved in the mission of the congregation.

All communicant members are automatically involved in the three business-service meetings of the congregation held each year and incorporated in a regular worship service. The carrying out of major goals and new decisions is left to the 11 functional committees and their working directors.

The new pastor was delighted with the planning done prior to his arrival. With his openness, insights, and concern for the people he won their confidence and helped members to further identify themselves personally with the desired goals. He recognized that a congregation's life stems from its sense of purpose and a clear understanding of its goals by its full membership.[10]

MULTIPLYING THE WORKERS

WE ARE ALL IN THIS TOGETHER

In a small church-related college in Edmondton, Alberta, there are two bronze plaques on the wall of the chapel-auditorium. On one is the profile of Dr. Martin Luther in low relief. On the other the likeness of Dr. C. F. W. Walther. Under each "portrait" are the words of 1 Peter 2:9, "You are a royal priesthood," the Scripture which was so significant to the great reformer and his American disciple. This apostolic word deserves a place in every Christian college and seminary if the coming generation of Christian leaders are to recover the principle and *practice* of the priesthood of all believers.[1]

If the church is to use this principle as a prototype, then every congregation in every age and place needs to be a mission station sending out its members on mission and service. *The pastor is a mission director and enabler. His team is as large as his congregation.*

However, the pastor is always in danger of accepting the image his people give him, intead of the fuller commission Christ has given him. He must beware of being pressed into a man-made or congregation—and community-made mold. He is not merely a representative of the people in preaching and administering the sacraments, or their substitute. This often means changing the congregation's image of itself, an image often short of the pattern left for us by the apostles and early Christians. That is why we have discussed the self-understanding of the layman. This involves the reorientation of all members, old and new. Tradition has a way of disfiguring the Biblical image. Pastor and people have a common ministry. What are the new priorities of the pastor if he is to activate all the people as fellow ministers? *Re-education is not an option. It is a necessity!*

How extensive is the mission and ministry of the people in your parish? How many are leaders and teachers in the church's educational agencies? On various working committees? How many have leadership positions among the youth? the adults? couples and families? How many are enlisted in *ongoing* evangelism?

More difficult is taking the measure of their Christian ministry in their daily work and in the community, business, civic, and social service sectors of their lives. To what extent are these "outside the parish services" recognized by the congregation? A congregational self-study with this kind of "camera" would be both revealing and in most cases heartening.

Begin with the personal interests of your members. Ask them to serve first where they now are, and in areas in which they are already interested. Then steer them into other and diverse areas of service. Let them experience how rewarding such service can be to the people they work with and to themselves personally. Give them opportunities to share their witness experience with a class, the evangelism committee, new members of the parish.

Today's pastors are called on to take so many roles and to be responsible for so many things. What comes first? preacher? teacher? organizer? strategist? deputizer? *The pastor can work alone; at his own pace; with his own preferences; according to what people and parishioners expect. But he will do so at the expense of his people, his community, and his Lord!*

He can greatly multiply the workers for Christ if he becomes God's "dispatcher," seeing in every person received into the parish many potentials. This takes more than premembership doctrinal instruction. It means finding each new member's talents and abilities, involving that person in some service for Christ. The pastor can do this with the help of assignment secretaries.

A WORKING FELLOWSHIP

Building the congregation into a "fellowship of the concerned" and a "company of the committed" is not easy. *But it is necessary* if a parish wishes to be more than a mere "holding operation." This cannot be achieved in the ordinary formal church service. But it can be awakened there, with preaching that stirs the heart and that challenges the mind to move from listener to worker. Personal service should be called for, not merely money offerings.

The reception of new members should include their orientation to the congregation's work program with its variety of services. Are new members related to other members in the parish living in the same neighborhood? A member family can have open house for the new family introducing other nearby families of the parish. These and other get-acquainted fellowship sessions should have an openness about them that makes new members feel the warmth and rewards of Christian unity and service. *Without such expressions new members will imitate the passivity of so many church people whose only participation is coming to the church service.*

Neighborhood adult study-discussion groups have proved to be the most viable form of developing spiritually growing, fruit-bearing branches of the church-tree. The number and kind of groups can vary greatly. Women's neighborhood circles have been very productive. But these do not include the men. Of course, such groups can be formed of couples just as well. An out-of-church-building meeting place is important in itself!

New members need orientation to functional Christianity. This can be given in a series of short courses offered in fall, winter, and spring. (See the five courses listed in the footnotes for this chapter.) Such study-action groups will arrest the tendency of making joining a church a "graduation" instead of a "commencement."[2]

One churchman speaking of this kind of training writes: "I am prepared to predict that if the small-group idea spreads so that a majority of our members experience it, they will discover that bearing witness at work, at home, or at play is just as important and just as much 'church' work as serving on the church council or teaching a church school class. They will also find that the problem of inactive members will be considerably reduced."[3]

Paul warns Timothy against persons who hold to the outward forms of religion but do not exercise its power in their own lives; who seem to listen to everybody but never really arrive at a working knowledge of the truth or put it to work in their own lives (2 Timothy 3:5,7). The Sermon on the Mount (Matthew 5-7) stresses religion in daily living. Jesus' story of the Good Samaritan is a story about us and for us.

American Christians have many opportunities to serve in evangelism crusades, youth projects, world relief, every member and neighborhood visitations, social service projects, and the like. Our danger is that we talk about so many tasks and discuss so many problems without ever doing much about them. It was *involvement* that our Lord not only taught but *practiced*.

Learning and doing are always combined in the Scouting program of boys and girls. Some churches have listed as many as 30 projects which Girl Scouts may undertake *to learn by doing*. Among these are such things as:

Reading the Bible and praying daily.

Making a written report on a world mission.

Ability in leading a group in prayer.

Listing full-time positions for women in the church.

Completing a service project over a four-month period.

It is by such concrete assignments that we move from learning to living.

Every Christian should be confronted with such questions as: What am I doing with my life? What legacy will my life leave? *What you do with your life is the highest kind of stewardship.* The frivolous and accidental use of our time is often amazing. Our priesthood gives us our greatest challenge! An old saying puts it this way: He who would leave footprints on the sands of time must wear work shoes!

Frequently a congregation will give a small book to new members as they are received. Almost every church publication house has some helpful titles to choose from. One such book speaks of the church as "God's joyful people—one in the spirit" and points out what it means to be "God's colony" making vital contributions to the world simply by being the church.[4]

MODERN MAN AND THE CHURCH'S MISSION

Erich Fromm, a social psychologist, speaks of the dilemma of modern man: "Our approach to life today becomes increasingly mechanical. Our main aim is to produce things, and in the process of this idolatry of things we transform ourselves into commodities. People are treated as numbers. . . . The question is whether people are things or living beings. . . . In giant centers of production, giant cities, great countries men are administered as if they were things. . . . But man is not meant to be a thing; he is destroyed if he becomes a thing; and before this is accomplished he becomes desperate and wants to kill all life. . . . People living in such a system become indifferent to life and even attracted to death.'"

There are other signs of the world's spiritual sickness: The mania for the creature comforts of life, the rebellion against old forms and moral standards, racism, the galloping increase of crimes, the restlessness of the people, militancy, corruption in high places. All of these are glaring examples of man's inhumanity to man.

These are symptoms of frustration. They are maladies that cannot be cured by a trip to the drugstore. They are signs our Lord asks us to observe. They are God's call to the church to go into action on an accelerated scale. Why? Because the Gospel has the answer! It alone provides reconciliation with man's Maker. It also brings reconciliation between man and man! For this world task the church needs an adequate strategy.

The Gospel gives a new relation to God, a new self-esteem, a new and greater purpose for life. It provides the philosophy of hope which modern man so desperately needs. People need an anchor for their lives. To reach modern man the full forces of the church are needed, both clergy and laity. Millions do not know "where they are" or "who they are." So great is their lostness! Christ came to seek and save them; to find, to heal, and to enlist them in His mission!

IN THE WORLD AND FOR THE WORLD

Jesus went out of His way to meet people of all sorts. He faced up to the scribes, Pharisees, and Sadducees. He met common people everywhere and entered into conversation with them. He lost no opportunity to call people winsomely to the new life. His last words to His disciples—and to every Christian—we call the great commission: "Go, then, to all peoples everywhere and make them My disciples!" (Matthew 28:19-20 TEV).

We cannot convert the world if we flee into our churches. Instead we are to be part of a continuous

Pentecost that reveals the Gospel in all manner of ways, to all people, to the end of time. We are not only to *speak* of our new hope, we are to *live* that hope!

The 19th century and the early 20th century saw great missionary expansions. Significant were the new fields entered after World War I and again after World War II. Vast new areas have been opened to the Gospel in Africa, India, South America, and the island empires of the Pacific. American and European churches made new explorations and developed significant mission and ministry strategies. However there were also some losses. Two world wars, political, social, and technological revolutions brought about what we might call a re-paganization of large populations. This situation calls for new evaluations and new strategies on the part of the church.

The priesthood of all believers is our greatest single hope for fulfilling God's mission. Christian laymen in the full generic sense of the term are already in dispersion throughout most of the world. However they are only partially equipped. So many have not been enlisted for their mission (to fulfill it where they are), or adequately trained. Only the full memberships of all Christian churches can fulfill the Lord's great commission.

The institutionalization of the church can become its grave. This is an extremely hard judgment. But it must be faced honestly. Restricting mission work to full-time Christian workers can so decimate the Lord's forces that only a holding operation is achievable. This is why the interdenominational mission conferences for half a century have called for a more adequate strategy.

We have already told the story of the church's mission in New Guinea. The secret of its rapid growth is due to the implementation of the priesthood-of-believers principle by children, youth, and adults.

A missionary on furlough from New Guinea evaluates the present situation for us:

In many respects New Guinea churches are falling into the mould of the western Churches, whereby an educated clergy assumes all responsibility. This trend is painfully recognized and efforts are being made to provide training for men in all conditions of life, so that they can relate their Christianity to their situation.

I have seen in New Guinea the erosion of some congregations at about the time a professional type of evangelist was in the process of being evolved. There are some other factors involved, such as the breakdown of the clan authority, younger people moving to full-time jobs away from home. Our big problem is to make all efforts in the direction of involving laity without any hint at forming a professional group in the American sense of the term. My next tour of duty in New Guinea is going to involve us directly in this task—to implement a mission policy embracing the priesthood of all believers.[6]

In the priesthood of all believers Christendom has an old prescription for a modern malady. The question is: Will the sick churches take this medicine? It may take hospitalization, the running of many tests, a surgical operation, and the rehabilitation of the body with a set of new spiritual exercises.

The real struggle of the world is spiritual. Political, economic, and social solutions are not getting at the core of the world's illness. Neither battlefield nor conference table have succeeded in giving man what he needs most.

THE COMBINED VOICE OF LAITY AND CLERGY

The persistent call to the churches of the world by directors and professors of missions in the last few decades has been for the activation of the laity.

"The best man to win another is the one who sits where he sits, the converted convict best wins other convicts; the farmer farmers; the factory worker factory workers. . . . Acceptance of Christian witness is the task of the entire membership of the church. The special responsibility of the layman is to bear such witness in the public life of the community, to set up signs of the kingdom in social righteousness and economic justice, as well as to take their share in the pastoral and evangelistic work of the church." This was the conclusion of the International Missionary Conference of 1952.[7]

Churchmen in every decade have alerted us. Robert McAfee Brown put it this way: "The true meaning of the Reformation phrase 'priesthood of the laity' is not that everybody is his own priest, so that no community is necessary; but rather that everybody must be a priest to everybody else, so that community is a necessity."[8]

We must not think that the priesthood of believers is restricted to the Protestant churches of the world. In 1946 Pius XII addressed these words to all Roman Catholics: "The faithful, and more precisely the laity, are stationed in the front ranks of the church, and through them the church is the living principle of human society. Consequently, they especially must have an even clearer consciousness, *not only of belonging to the church, but of being the church.*"

In 1957 some 30,000 delegates from 86 countries of the world met in Rome in the second World Congress of the Lay Apostolate. The mission of the church to the world, it was said, cannot be fulfilled by washing our hands in innocence of the world but by penetrating that world as witnesses to the Christian message. The secular world, all of it, is the mission territory of the lay Christian. This world can be penetrated for Christ "only if we [laymen] do it." It will need to happen on the streets, in offices and shops, in our homes, over the backyard fence, in our daily contact with men.

An American bishop, John Wright, in 1960 put the call in these words: "When men and women of their own background, class, and condition speak up with the mind and heart of the church, Christ has a chance to be heard more readily and effectively. What is special about our times is this: God's message for the world and the contribution of the church to society will be taken best, when at all, from convinced laymen rather than from the official teachers of the church.'"

MULTIPLYING THE WORKERS

Few American churchmen have made greater contributions to the enlistment and training of the laity than John Raleigh Mott over the period of his long and fruitful life (1865 to 1955). He is considered one of the greats in world Protestant leadership in the field of missions. He has rightly been called "Layman Extraordinary." It was he who gave Christendom a new vision in a single sentence: *"Greater is he that multiplies the workers than he who does the work."* This is a rephrasing of Samuel Morley's dictum: "He who does the work is not so profitably employed as he who multiplies the doers." Dwight L. Moody put it into a similar phrase: "It's better to put ten men to work than to do the work of ten men."

One wishes these phrases were Biblical. In essence they actually are. Jesus operated with this principle. He selected 12 men. He went before them for 3 years showing what the ministry of the new age should be like. He established no formal seminary. Yet every theological seminary in the world draws on the principle: "Multiply the workers." But more than that, every pastor who follows Christ's principle of sending out the Twelve and the Seventy is using the only pattern that has any chance of fulfilling the great commission.

Dr. Mott began each day with his Bible. One day he came upon the words of Jesus in John 17:16-17, "What I teach is not Mine, but comes from God, who sent Me. Whoever is willing to do what God wants will know whether what I teach comes from God or whether I speak on My own authority." Of this verse Mott said, "God directed it straight at me! It gave me assured faith in Jesus, not only as the Son of God, but as my personal Savior. It tore me loose from every plan, sent me to Ceylon, later to India, and kept me hard at Christian service throughout my life."[10]

From the time when he himself was recruited to the service of the kingdom of God as a student at Cornell University he kept at his first task: calling youth to the same high adventure. His energy, all the weapons of his armament, each talent he possessed, and the majority of his working hours were harnessed to this task of enlisting workers for Christ. He often said, "Recruiting is the most important single thing I have to do." He was constantly discovering, enlisting, training, and opening up avenues of service for Christian workers. Toward the close of his career Dr. Mott said: "Nor would I by one iota change that emphasis if I had my life to live over again."[11] His favorite quote was, "Pray the Lord of the harvest that He send forth laborers into His harvest."

John R. Mott enlisted people (mostly laymen) for Christ's mission on every continent. The demand for his leadership was worldwide. He said it was his constant endeavor not to let a day pass without confronting someone with the living Christ. The well-known American church historian Kenneth Scott Latourette said: "No one since the days of St. Paul has done so much to spread the Gospel of Jesus Christ as Dr. Mott." This layman extraordinary had a great vision and tremendous organizing ability. Christian youth were drawn to him everywhere and prominent church leaders went to him for counsel and direction. He was immensely practical, not theoretical. He helped to develop a "cloud of witnesses" (Hebrews 12:1).

The vision of this man of God is revealed in his seven principles here cited in condensed form:

(1) Make universities and colleges enlistment and propagating centers for vital Christianity.

(2) Develop and liberate the limitless but latent forces of Christianity.

(3) Confront young men and women with the living Christ.

(4) Begin the day with God and live it as though it were your last.

(5) Organize and distribute God's forces advantageously as His servant.

(6) *Multiply the workers. This is a first priority.*

(7) Expand the forces of Christianity so that more people in each generation can hear the Christian message.[12]

Christian renewal begins locally—in *your* congregation. And it begins personally—in your own mind and life. That has been the message of these chapters.

In every generation, in every decade, in every congregation, in every church body the New Testament polity needs to be rediscovered and given implementation. In many ways this is obvious. We can learn the lesson from the ants, the bees, and from the cell structure of plants. This wisdom of the Creator is to be applied in practice by the redeemed, called, and commissioned people of God.

In one of his lectures, John Raleigh Mott put the challenge into these bold, forceful words: "A multitude of laymen are today in serious danger. It is positively perilous for them to hear more sermons, attend more Bible classes, open forums, and read more religious and ethical works, unless accompanying it all there be afforded day by day an adequate outlet for their new found faith."[13]

He that multiplies the workers is greater than he who does the work! This is God's basic strategy for the churches of the New Covenant. We, the chosen people of God, must implement it. It is a matter of life and breath!

Jesus put this into a single sentence on the day He ascended to heaven: "You shall receive power when the Holy Spirit has come upon you; and YOU shall be My witnesses in Jerusalem, and in all Judea and Samaria and to the end of the earth!" (Acts 1:18).

THE GIST OF THIS BOOK

"Mission and ministry" as it grows out of a fresh look at the New Testament means all of God's people exercising their spiritual priesthood every day wherever they are—in all the contact and service areas of life, in their daily occupation, in formal and informal associations with people. The New Testament gives us six terms which help us rediscover the scope and nature of this ministry. To be the church means: All Christians are sent to our age to infect all society with the liberating, saving, ministering power of the Gospel of Jesus Christ; adults, youth, children, forming a witnessing team, not only by what they say but by what they are!

The exercise of this universal priesthood does not do away with the institutional church or the necessity of the pastoral office. It is a God-ordained basic means to multiply the church's ministry by utilizing the full membership of a parish; it is carried out not only in the church edifice, but in the family, the neighborhood, the community, in fact, throughout the world wherever there are disciples of Jesus Christ; in this way it fulfills the great commission which Christ gives to all who accept Him as Savior and Lord.

This is not a new doctrine, but the repristination of the early church and a recovery of the Reformation principle of being a witness to Christ in every arena of life.

FOOTNOTES

CHAPTER ONE

[1]Hans Küng, *Why Priests? A Proposal for a New Church Ministry*, (Garden City, N.Y.: Doubleday, 1972) trans. from German by R. C. Collins, S.J., 118 pages, introduction.

[2]*Forum Letter* (American Lutheran Publicity Bureau), ed. Richard E. Koenig, Jan. 1973, p. 4.

[3]Albert McClellan, *The New Times, A Prophetic Look at the Challenge to the Christian Church in the 1970s* (Nashville: Broadman, 1968), 128 pp.

[4]*Küng*, pp. 13, 17, 23.

[5]For more details see David S. Schuller, *Emerging Shapes of the Church* (St. Louis: Concordia, 1967).

CHAPTER TWO

[1]"Mission Affirmation," 1965, adopted by the Lutheran Church—Missouri Synod. Similar statements have been drawn up by other church bodies and church councils.

[2]*Worker-Priest* Bibliography: The worker-priest pattern was developed mainly in France. See articles in *The Christian Century:* 4/21/71; 2/16/72, in *Commonweal:* from 1954 onward; also 1973 Research Project and Syllabus by Victor Hafner, Concordia Seminary, St. Louis, Mo.

[3]*Key '73, Congressional Resource Book,* "Calling Our Continent to Christ," pp. 243. T. A. Raedeke, executive director. An outline of the comprehensive 6 phases, referred to as "the greatest thing that has happened to the church since the Reformation," are available from denominational headquarters.

[4]D. James Kennedy, *Evangelism Explosion* (Wheaton, Ill.: Tyndale House Publishers, 1970).

[5]Ralph D. Winter, *The 25 Unbelievable Years: 1945–1969,* (Wm. Carey Library 533 Hermosa St., South Pasadena, Calif. 91030), pp. 55, 61, 121, 124; chs. 2, 3, 4.

[6]Manoel de Mello, "Participation is Everything," an article in *International Review of Missions*, LX, 238 (April 1971), 245–48.

[7]"Report of the Latin American Team," May 1971, 20 pp., distributed by Lutheran Council of the USA, 315 Park Ave. South, New York, N.Y. 10010; on greater lay participation in the church's worship and pastoral life: pp. 11, 12, 16, 17.

[8]So reported by Fred Pankow, Secretary for Latin America, The Lutheran Church—Missouri Synod.

[9]Winter, *"The 25 Unbelievable Years 1945–1969,"* pp. 16, 21, 61, 121–125; Barrett quotation, p. 28. Also consult: Kenneth Latourette's *A History of the Expansion of Christianity* (7 vols.) and *Christianity in a Revolutionary Age* (5 vols).

[10]Winter, p. 61.

[11]*Church Growth Bulletin,* 305 Pasadena Ave., South Pasadena, Calif. 91030.

[12]Winter, pp. 125–26, 106–11.

[13]Edwin Lueker, *Change and the Church* (St. Louis: Concordia, 1969), pp. 44–45.

[14]K. Birdston, "A Younger Church in Stormy Seas," *Lutheran World,* Spring, 1955.

[15]Lueker, p. 118.

[16]Winter, pp. 1, 99, 106–8.

[17]For additional up-to date materials on this most recent missionary advance write for: "The Church Growth Book Club Bulletin," Jan. 1973, 305 Pasadena Ave., South Pasadena, Calif. 91030. Note such titles as: Wm. R. Read, *Latin American Church Growth,* (Eerdmans, 1969); Read, *New Patterns of Church Growth in Brazil,* (Eerdmans, 1965); C. P. Wagner, *The Protestant Movement in Bolivia,* (William Carey Library, 1970) For an interesting new diagnostic approach to three kinds of church growth (conversion, transfers in, and biological growth-children born into Christian families) see Vergel Gerber's *A Manual for Evangelism/Church Growth,* 1973, published by William Carey Library, 533 Hermosa St., South Pasadena, Calif. 91030. 95 pp. See article "The Only Hope for World Evangelism" by David A. Womack, in *Christianity Today,* July 20, 1973.

CHAPTER THREE

Books cited in Chapter Three in order of appearance.

[1]All of Trueblood's books, including his *Abraham Lincoln—Theologian of American Anguish* (1973), are published by Harper and Row.

[2]James D. Smart, *The Teaching Ministry of the Church,* (Philadelphia: Westminster, 1954), pp. 92–95.

[3]Wallace A. Fischer, *From Tradition to Mission* (Nashville: Abingdon, 1965).

⁴Howard Grimes, *The Rebirth of the Laity* (Nashville, Abingdon, 1962).

⁵Francis O. Ayres, *The Ministry of the Laity* (Philadelphia: Westminster, 1962), p. 132.

⁶Douglas Webster, *Local Church and World Mission* (New York: Seabury, 1964), p. 48, 50, 8.

⁷Daniel D. Walker, *Enemy in the Pew?* (New York: Harper and Row, 1967), p. 140; chs. 6, 7, 8.

⁸Jeffrey K. Hadden, *The Gathering Storm in the Churches* (Garden City, N.Y.: Doubleday, 1969), pp. 29–30, 228, 231.

⁹David Poling, *The Last Years of the Church* (Garden City, N.Y.: Doubleday, 1969), p. 67, 71, 144.

¹⁰E. Glenn Hinson, *The Church: Design for Survival* (Nashville: Broadman, 1967), chs. 1, 3, 7, 8.

¹¹Donald L. Metz, *New Congregations, Security and Mission in Conflict* (Philadelphia: Westminster, 1967), ch. 9.

¹²Russell Bow, *The Integrity of Church Membership* (Waco, Tex.: Word Books, 1968), p. 89; chs. 1–2.

¹³Merle A. Johnson, *Beyond Enchantment* (Old Tappan, N.J.: Revell, 1972).

¹⁴Robert S. Clemmons, *Education for Churchmanship* (Nashville: Abingdon, 1966), ch. 2.

¹⁵William M. Ramsay, *Cycles of Renewal* (Nashville: Abingdon, 1969), pp. 18, 34–41, 130.

¹⁶Erwin Lueker, *Change and the Church*, (St. Louis: Concordia, 1969), pp. 49–50, 118.

¹⁷Robert C. Worley, *Change in the Church: A Source of Hope* (Philadelphia: Westminster, 1971).

Other Books:

Elizabeth O'Connor, *Call to Committment* (New York: Harper and Row, 1963).

Stephen Rose, *The Grass Roots Church* (Nashville: Abingdon, 1968).

George W. Webber, *The Congregation in Mission* (Nashville: Abingdon, 1964).

CHAPTER FOUR

¹J. B. Philipps, *The Young Church in Action* (New York: MacMillan, 1955), p. vii.

²Dr. Philip Schaff (1819 to 1893), professor of church history, Union Theological Seminary (1877). Author of 7 vol. *History of the Christian Church* (1892), *Creeds of Christendom* (1877); Editor, Schaff-Herzog *Encyclopedia of Religious Knowledge* (1880); as quoted from Schaff's *Luther as a Reformer* in *Four Hundred Years* (St. Louis: Concordia, 1917), p. 291.

³Schaff, as quoted in *Four Hundred Years*, p. 302 f.

⁴William Dallman, in a chapter on "Justification by Faith," *Four Hundred Years*, p. 70. Also see: "Luthers View of Be-

liever-Priests in the Church," *Christianity Today*, Oct. 26, 1973.

⁵C. Abbetmeyer, in a chapter on "Formation-Deformation-Reformation," *Four Hundred Years*, p. 3.

⁶Franklin Littell, professor of church history, Temple University, Philadelphia, Pa.

⁷Elton Trueblood, *Your Other Vocation* (New York: Harper and Row, 1952), p. 52.

⁸William J. Danker, in *Concordia Theological Monthly*, Sept. 1960.

⁹R. C. Halverson, in *Christianity Today*, Sept. 12, 1960.

¹⁰In examining a number of Christian catechisms and adult premembership instruction manuals no mention of, or wholly inadequate reference to, the priesthood of all believers was found.

CHAPTER FIVE

¹Paul S. Minear, *Jesus and His People* (New York: Association Press, 1956), 93 pp. *Images of the Church in the New Testament* (Philadelphia: Westminster, 1960), 294 pp.

²Cyril Eastwood, *The Priesthood of All Believers* (Minneapolis: Augsburg, 1962), 268 pp.

³Ibid., pp. 60, 87, 199.

⁴Ibid., p. 100.

⁵Ibid., p. 125.

⁶Ibid., p. 127.

⁷Ibid., p. 128.

⁸Ibid., p. 144.

⁹Ibid., p. 146.

¹⁰Ibid., p. 155; see also *The Works of John Smyth*.

¹¹Ibid., p. 199; see also *New History of Methodism*, Townsend and Workman, I, pp. 5–6.

¹²Ibid., Introduction, p. IX.

¹³Ibid., ch. 6, pp. 238–57. The summary theses are those of Dr. Eastwood. The commentary which follows includes thoughts from Eastwood, but usually supply comments by the writer of this book. Eastwood's statements are shown in quotations.

¹⁴Ibid., pp. 246–47.

¹⁵The references here are mostly condensations.

¹⁶Küng, pp. 35, 28.

¹⁷Ibid., pp. 33–34.

¹⁸Ibid., pp. 39–40, 46–48.

¹⁹Ibid., p. 58.

²⁰Ibid., p. 115.

²¹Ibid., p. 34

²²Ibid., p. 42.

²³Ibid., p. 78

²⁴Ibid., p. 103.

CHAPTER SIX

[1]In 1 Corinthians 1:2, 26 four Greek terms related to *kaleo* (to call) are used; in Ephesians 4:1, 4, four similar terms; in 2 Timothy 1:9, two such terms.

[2]William Robinson, *Completing the Reformation: The Doctrine of the Priesthood of All Believers*, a series of lectures at Lexington (Ky.) Theological Seminary delivered in 1955; 70 pages; p. 20.

[3]Elton Trueblood, *Your Other Vocation* (New York: Harper and Row, 1952), pp. 29–30. *The Company of the Committed* (New York: Harper and Row, 1961), 113 pages.

[4]Hendrick Kraemer, *A Theology of the Laity* (Philadelphia: Westminster, 1958), pp. 51–55. Francis O. Ayres, *The Ministry of the Laity* (Philadelphia: Westminster, 1962), pp. 13–33. Howard Grimes, *The Church Redemptive* (Nashville: Abingdon, 1958), ch. 3; pp. 35–46, 62. *The Rebirth of the Laity* (Nashville: Abingdon, 1962), ch. 5; pp. 50–51.

[5]J. B. Lightfoot: see his classical "Dissertation on the Christian Ministry" in his commentary on Philippians, 1868.

[6]Read the six-page article "Minister, Ministry" in Alan Richardson's *A Theological Word Book to the Bible* (New York: MacMillan, 1962 , paperback pp. 146–152.

[7]*The Church and the Changing Ministry*, a study by the United Presbyterian Church, R. C. Johnson, ed. 1961, pp. 22–59 (Philadelphia)

[8]Robinson, pp. 14–15.

[9]Richard R. Cæmmerer and Erwin L. Lueker, *The Church and Ministry in Transition: (Application of Scripture and History to Current Questions)* (St. Louis: Concordia, 1964), 80 pp; p. 62, 66.

[10]William Dallmann, in *Four Hundred Years*, p. 70.

[11]Küng. pp. 46–49.

[12]Ole Christian Hallesby († 1961) Oslo, Norway; professor of the Independent Theological Seminary for 40 years.

[13]Albert McClellan, *The New Times: A Prophetic Look at the Challenge to the Christian Church in the 1970s* (Nashville: Broadman, 1968), p. 113.

[14]E. Glenn Hinson, *The Church: Design for Survival* (Nashville: Broadman, 1967), p. 95.

CHAPTER SEVEN

[1]Donald R. Heiges, *The Christian's Calling* (Philadelphia: Muhlenberg Press, 1958), 114 pp; pp. 4–5.

[2]Abbreviated from Heiges, p. 11.

[3]Heiges, p. 83.

[4]This is the dynamic which the Gospel provides.

[5]Heiges, p. 32.

[6]Heiges, p. 60. See Luther's six criteria for Christian vocation. At Luther's time persons who lived in the celibate orders were considered to have the perfect form of Christian life. Those who married and reared children or had a "secular" calling were regarded as having a secondary, lower grade of piety. Against this Luther rebelled. Ibid. pp. 41–45.

[7]Gustaf Wingren, "The Christian's Calling According to Luther," *Augustana Quarterly* (Oct. 1947), XXVI, 4.

[8]*Your Human Rights: The Universal Declaration of Human Rights*, United Nations 1948 (71 p. booklet, Ellner, Inc. 1950).

[9]McClellan, p. 108.

[10]Ibid., p. 109.

[11]David Schuller, *The New Urban Society*, p. 94. (St. Louis: Concordia, 1966) chs. 3 and 6.

[12]T. A. Kantonen, *The Resurgence of the Gospel* (Philadelphia: Muhlenberg, 1948), p. 94.

[13]Martin Luther, quoted in *Theological Foundations of Bible Study, Train Two Leaders Manual*, Board of Parish Education, The Lutheran Church-Missouri Synod, p. 25.

[14]Richard C. Halverson, *"The Tragedy of the Unemployed,"* *Christianity Today*, IV, 25; (Sept. 12, 1960), pp. 9–10.

[15]Roy W. Fairchild and John Charles Wynn *Families in the Church: A Protestant Survey* (New York: Association Press, 1961), p. 94.

[16]Kraemer, p. 161. See also pp. 180–188. (Kraemer's book is a basic text which should be in every church library and which every pastor and layman should read.)

[17]In addition to Heiges and Kraemer also see Alexander Miller, *Christian Faith and My Job* (New York: Association Press, Reflection Book, 1959), p. 128.

CHAPTER EIGHT

[1]Kenneth L. Cober, *The Church's Teaching Ministry* (Valley Forge, Pa.: Judson, 1964) p. 31.

[2]For a more comprehensive and outstanding treatment of the key concepts of "ministry" in the New Testament see Cober's book: ch. 2, pp. 23–38.

[3]William Barclay, *Train Up a Child* (Philadelphia: Westminster, 1959), pp. 236, 262.

[4]William Kottmeyer, in *Letter to Parents*, St. Louis Board of Education, Dec. 1968.

[5]Edith Hunter, in *Religious Education,"* LII (March-April 1957), pp. 94-97.

[6]Edward and Harriet Dowdy, *The Church is Families* (Valley Forge, Pa.: Judson, 1965), pp. 15–16.

[7]Foundation Paper VI, 1961, Presbyterian Board of Education, Richmond, Va.

[8]Kraemer, p. 163.

[9]George W. Webber, *The Congregation in Mission* (Nashville; Abingdon, 1968) ch. 7–8.

[10]Ibid., p. 119.

[11]"Church Renewal—Outside the Structure," in *Christian Advocate*, Sept. 12, 1963, p. 10.

[12]D. James Kennedy, *Evangelism Explosion* (Wheaton, Ill.: Tyndale House, 1970), pp. 1–7.

[13]As reported by Paul J. Foust, Evangelism Counselor, Michigan District of the Lutheran Church—Missouri Synod. The men who initiated the program were the pastors of the Bethlehem Church, Saginaw, Mich.: Darrell M. Lubben, Jerold L. Nichols.

[14]Carey Moore, "Great Churches of Today," in *Decision Magazine*, Minneapolis, Minn., Feb. 1972.

[15]McClellan, pp. 122–127, 58–63.

[16]Henry P. Van Dusen, clergyman, editor of *Christianity and Crises*, 1945–1948

Note: The Scriptures and commentary in this and the next chapter can be used in your Bible classes and in the orientation training of new church members.

CHAPTER NINE

[1]Samuel Blizzard, "The Training of the Parish Minister," *Union Seminary Quarterly Review* (New York), XI, 2, p. 47.

[2]David J. Ernsberger, *A Philosophy of Adult Christian Education,* (Philadelphia: Westminster, 1959), p. 45–46.

[3]Ibid. ch. 2 and 3.

[4]Said by Robert Stackel, a member of the Executive Council, Lutheran Church in America.

[5]In the article "Put the Church into the World," *The Lutheran,* Periodical of Lutheran Church in America, Philadelphia, Pa., Jan. 24, 1962.

[6]Cober, p. 101.

[7]William Hinson, quoted by Harold H. Martin in his article "The American Minister—A National Report on the New Protestant Clergyman—His Troubles, His Triumphs," *The Saturday Evening Post,* April 24, 1965, p. 89

[8]James D. Smart, *The Rebirth of Ministry,* (Philadelphia: Westminster, 1960), p. 93.

[9]Ibid., p. 98.

[10]See "Kingdom Work in New Guinea," by Jeannelle Hintze, *Lutheran Woman's Quarterly,* XI, 4 (Oct. 1953), p. 3ff.

[11]"The Only Hope for World Evangelization," *Christianity Today,* July 20, 1973, p. 12.

[12]W. Leroy Biesenthal, Director of Stewardship and Evangelism, Missouri District of The Lutheran Church—Missouri Synod, has conducted clinics with students from two seminaries, in

close cooperation with the departments of practical theology at both schools. Clinics for pastors using the same techniques were conducted in other Districts.

[13]The Commission on Mission and Ministry, The Lutheran Church—Missouri Synod, St. Louis, Mo., 1969 report.

CHAPTER TEN

[1]Ceal Andre, at conference of District Christian Education Executives, St. Louis, Mo., Jan. 24, 1972.

[2]Richard C. Halverson, "The Tragedy of the Unemployed," *Christianity Today*, Sept. 12, 1960.

[3]Schuller, pp. 48–49.

[4]Ceal Andre, at occasion noted above.

[5]Timothy Lutheran Church, Paul Spitz, pastor, St. Louis, Mo.

[6]*A Team Ministry Approach for Multiple Rural Parishes*, printed proceedings (48 pp.) of a workshop at Grace Lutheran Church, Regina, Sask., April 1965. Convened by T. L. Ristine.

[7]McClellan, p. 109.

[8]Bernard M. Christensen, president of Augsburg Seminary, Minneapolis, (1938–1962), and author of *Fire Upon the Earth*.

Note: For more helpful suggestions on the use of volunteers in the church consult *The Christian Ministry*, May 1973, Christian Century Foundation, 407 So. Dearborn St., Chicago, Ill. 60605. This issue contains significant articles on working with volunteers, team ministries, recruiting laity.

CHAPTER ELEVEN

[1]Kraemer, p. 177

[2]Gerald J. Jud, in *Tempo Magazine*, Jan. 1969, p. 4–5.

[3]James Mayer, as quoted by Caemmerer and Lueker in *Church and Ministry in Transition*, pp. 12–14.

[4]Caemmerer and Lueker, pp. 15–16, 34, 54–56.

[5]Conrad Bergendoff, *The Church of the Lutheran Reformation* (St. Louis: Concordia, 1967), pp. 297–98.

[6]See Cober, p. 124. He suggests six significant goals in evaluating your parish.

[7]J. Donald Butler, *Religious Education—The Foundation and Practice of Nurture*, (New York: Harper and Row, 1962), pp. 280–81.

[8]This issue of the magazine devotes 40 pages to measuring ministries, resources for evaluation, planned self-appraisal, congregational self-evaluation, competency in the parish ministry, purpose, etc.; R. R. Broholm, *Strategic Planning for Church Organizations* (Valley Forge, Pa.: Judson, 1969), p. 32; Wm. F. Haase, *More Effective Church Boards and Committees*, National Council of Churches, 1966) p. 64; R. C. Rein, *The Congregation at Work* (St. Louis: Concordia, 1962), p. 247; H. J. Sweet,

The Multiple Staff in the Local Church (Philadelphia: Westminster, 1963), p. 122.

[9]See Worley, chs. 6–9.

[10]This description is the 1972–1973 experience of Trinity Lutheran Church, East St. Louis, Ill.

CHAPTER TWELVE

[1]C. F. W. Walther was the theological leader of a group of Saxon immigrants who came to America to secure religious liberty. He founded The Lutheran Church—Missouri Synod in 1847, served as its first president, and for many years was president of Concordia Seminary, St. Louis, Mo.

[2]A series of five reading-study books called *The Discipleship Series,*
(Concordia Publishing House, 1969–1971) supply basic training in functional Christianity.
(1) *Learning to Use Your Bible:* supplies a better background for reading, understanding, studying the Bible; 176 pp.
(2) *Christians Worship:* (worship helps us deepen our faith and equips us for Christian living); 146 pp.
(3) *The Christian's Mission:* personal guidance for personal witness in all arenas of life; 96 pp.
(4) *Christian Family Living:* faith is woven into the warp and woof of our lives in the Christ-centered home; 122 pp.
(5) *The Church Since Pentecost:* bridges the 19-century gap since the New Testament was written; 101 pp.

[3]J. Bruce Weaver, in article in *The Lutheran,* Jan. 24, 1962.

[4]Oswald C. J. Hoffman, *God's Joyful People—One in Spirit* (St. Louis: Concordia, 1973), 103 pp.

[5]Erich Fromm, *The Heart of Man* (New York: Harper and Row, 1968), paperback.

[6]An oral report by Missionary Karl Stotik on furlough in America, (May 1972).

[7]International Missionary Conference, 1952, Willigen; quoted in *Concordia Theological Monthly,* XXXI (Sept. 9, 1960), p. 550.

[8]Robert McAfee Brown, *Patterns of Faith Today,* ed. F. E. Johnson, 1957.

[9]From an address to the students of Xavier University, Cincinnati, O., 1960.

[10]John R. Mott, in *The Future Leadership of the Church,* (New York: YMCA, 1909), pp. 330–39.

[11]Basil Mathews in *John R. Mott, World Citizen,* (New York: Harper and Row, 1934), p. 332.

[12]Robert C. Mackie and others, *Laymen Extraordinary,* (New York: Association Press, 1965), pp. 101–02.

[13]John R. Mott authored 13 books, edited 5 other books, wrote hundreds of articles, reports, and pamphlets, One seminary library has 22 cards in its index on Dr. Mott and his work.